Michael,
Don't go into the cemetery at night
You might f

True Tales From a Cemetery Cop

Jaimie Vernon

© 2016 Jaimie Vernon
Bullseye Canada Publishing
Toronto, Ontario, Canada

All rights reserved.
Unauthorized duplication is strictly prohibited.
The name Cemetery Cop, the motto "to serve and protect the dead" and the badge logo are trademarks of Bullseye.

Photographs and cover art by Jaimie Vernon

ISBN-13: 978-1537138022

Dedicated to:

Wendy Barker (1964 – 1975)
Lauretta Vernon (1944 – 1976)
Joseph "Larry" Hains (1902 – 1979)
George Robertson (1934 – 1982)
Gladys Smithson (1897 – 1982)
Herbert Barker (1915 – 1984)
Shierene Vernon (1917 – 1990)
Lillian Vernon (1925 – 2000)
Jean Vernon (1938 – 2004)
Sam Vernon (1910 – 2005)
Linda Gifkins (1941 – 2006)
Jim Gifkins (1940 – 2007)
James Vernon (1939 – 2007)
Spencer Vernon (1913 – 2008)
John Vernon (1937 – 2011)
Marge Barker (1916 – 2011)
Brenda Barker (1963 – 2015)
Kariann Ford (1967 – 2016)

*"If any of you cry at my funeral,
I'll never speak to you again."
– Stan Laurel*

CONTENTS

Acknowledgments	i
Introduction	3
Chapter One	6
Chapter Two	12
Chapter Three	24
Chapter Four	33
Chapter Five	41
Chapter Six	53
Chapter Seven	65
Chapter Eight	75
Chapter Nine	99
Chapter Ten	122
Chapter Eleven	141
Chapter Twelve	151

ACKNOWLEDGMENTS

To Sharon, Riley and Danielle who stuck by me despite enduring a year without me as I worked shifts beyond exhaustion and tried my best to be 'normal' when I got home. I know you sacrificed a lot. Love you.

To the security crew who had my back…and front. Thanks for accepting me as one of you.

To the various cemetery staffs who treated me with courtesy and respect. Glad I could be there for you.

To Barb DiGiulio whose 'Nightside' radio show was warm comfort on cold, dark nights amongst the unliving.

To Kris Abbott & Dee McNeil whose songs on the '*A Great Long Game*' CD saved my life. You can never know how deeply they changed my world view.

To Simon Bedford-James for facilitating my ability to get a security guard license.

INTRODUCTION

Becoming a security guard was never a vocation, it was a necessity at the heels of a long line of jobs I had to take for the sake of food and shelter during the 21st century's economic meltdown. Had I been inclined to live outdoors or looking to knock a few pounds off from lack of sustenance I'd be writing a different story altogether. As it turned out, what started as a run-of-the-mill stop-gap paycheque became an eye opening experience of seeing life, and death, from a whole different perspective.

I've done a lot of jobs in my life - janitor, car wash attendant, census taker, government archivist, mailroom clerk, warehouse worker, radio tracker, graphic designer, musician, record label president and even a professional car driver. Never have I done a job that mattered on a human, emotional level.

Working security at one of the busiest cemeteries in the middle of a major city is not for the faint of heart. The work is not difficult as such - though sitting in a patrol car is unusually tiring in 15 hour stretches - so it might come as a surprise to learn that it boasts a level of responsibility and empathy you would never see written in a job description.

I've put up a strong facade of being the stoic tough guy in public, but it's difficult to remain aloof and detached when you deal mostly with people who are living through the worst days of their lives. You realize quickly that when you set aside everyone's differing beliefs, social status and dreams that we all have one thing in common - death. It's inescapable. Everyone gets the same cubic footage six feet under – or through the miracle of science – a two cubic foot curio cabinet to spend the rest of eternity in.

My interaction with grieving families paled in comparison to the cemetery staff I answered to on a daily basis. The funeral support staff possess a constitution that can only be described as a true calling. I can't imagine how much you must love what you do to have to walk people through the most painful time of their lives; facing unbridled anger and heartbreak - usually at the same time. I couldn't do it. The burnout level and PTSD for undertakers and funeral directors must be huge.

That's why they do what they do and I did the rest - protecting the dead from the living. I had no horse in their race and was sent into these hallowed grounds as a sentry because despite the presumption of peace and tranquility, cemeteries are anything but.

When I've told people what I used to do for a living the first cliché that springs to ones lips is invariably "Were people dying to get in?" My response always surprised them, "No. People were desperate to get out!"

The look I would receive was worth the response. The life journey is over for the deceased when their remains pass through the gates of the cemetery and consequently the anguish begins immediately for the survivors. Simultaneously, there were also visitors to the cemetery. Those who, for whatever reason, found solace or a twisted dark interest in both the scenery and energy found in such places. And when I locked the gates at sundown, the panic would begin. Without exception all visitors wanted out of the cemetery and they wanted out NOW.

The second question people ask me about the work I did is "Why do they need security at graveyards? Everyone's dead." It's true. I never had a problem with anyone interred there. My primary job was to protect the dead from harm and it's that pretense that led to writing this book.

The stories, on the surface, seem incredible to many. I have no doubt that you may think that while reading them. All of these tales are true. They are my stories as I observed them as was expected of me in my job. In comparing notes with other guards in my squad there were even more, so many more. Maybe one day I can collect those into a book as well but for now I present a year in the life of one cemetery cop.

Jaimie Vernon
September 2016

The names contained herein have been changed to protect the privacy of the living. The cemetery referred to is a composite of the many places I had to patrol during my duties as a security guard and shall remain anonymous to protect the privacy of the dead, and the confidentiality of my former employer, the cemeteries and their staff respectively. All opinions are mine and not those of the security industry or the funeral industry.

*** WARNING: THIS BOOK CONTAINS GRAPHIC DESCRIPTIONS OF FUNERALS, DEATH AND HUMAN REMAINS ***

CHAPTER ONE

FROM RAIL YARD TO GRAVE YARD

Through social conditioning we grow up to view cemeteries superstitiously via religion or the urban legends concocted and repeated in the medium of television and movies. We have learned to believe that the souls of the dead and/or the zombie apocalypse will rise from every graveyard. It's this pathological fear of the dead, dark places and ghosts that landed me the job I ended up doing for an entire year.

I had just been fired from my full-time gig as an auto-inspector at one of the largest rail yards in Canada. That was my official job description but during the majority of 2014 management had changed at the facility where I was inspecting and shuttling Chrysler automobiles and I found myself doing other people's jobs more than my own. They had systematically fired a dozen workers in as many months and everyone that was left was stuck covering the work that remained.

To that end we were exhausted. 12-14 hour shifts with

no days off for weeks at a time. There were so many human rights violations it was maddening. But everyone was afraid of losing their jobs. We were still in post-2008 recession recovery. Besides, the overtime pay was outrageous. No one wanted to lose that. So we endured near death experiences.

I had mine in August of 2014.

If you've ever been a parent and sleep deprived because your kid hasn't slept in 3 years, that was me. I'd done 17 days straight without time off. I was seeing double. I was losing track of time. Huge chunks of time. No one who is sleep deprived should be driving automobiles for a living. Even if it's in a secured facility and away from the general public.

I was moving a brand new 2015 Honda Odyssey mini-van from a holding area parking lot over to a staging area where a waiting transport truck would take it and several other vehicles to its final destination at some area car dealership. It never made it there. I pulled into the common area in the yard where a dozen other drivers were doing the same. I blanked out as I pulled into yard traffic and drove directly into an approaching GMC pick-up truck. It wasn't very fast as I had already stopped to make the turn. But the truck was doing the requisite 20km/h and I was a brick wall. The front end of both vehicles were destroyed.

I suffered a concussion as the airbag hit me in the chest – not in the face because we never applied seatbelts during these 90 second guerilla shuttle runs. It was impractical. My head took the brunt of it on the windshield. The top of my head was bleeding. The horn on the mini-van was stuck open. The entire yard heard what was going on.

The new supervising manager ran out and helped disconnect the horn. Then yelled at me. He wanted to know if I wanted to go to the hospital. I was angry. Angry that I had now destroyed my driving record and angry that it was because of this irresponsible slave driver.

I was instead taken home until I'd recovered from my head injury. I was watched intently by my wife over the next three days. On the fourth day they called me in to discuss my future. I was fired when I walked through the door.

I should have fought them. I should have taken them to court for every violation I'd documented after they'd brought in this new management team. Instead, I thanked them. Thanked them for letting me out of the nightmare I'd been enduring for two years. I hadn't had a good night's sleep in that long. I'd lost 35 pounds from walking 12,000 to 15,000 steps a day. I was malnourished and was suffering serious hallucinations on a daily basis. They did me a favour. I was free.

And I was unemployed. The government frowns on people being fired even with an explanation. I couldn't collect unemployment benefits. I needed to get back to work pronto.

It would mean getting out of dungarees, overalls and work boots and putting on a shirt, pants and a decent pair of shoes. I didn't own a decent pair of shoes because I'd been wearing work boots continuously for two years. I went shopping at a local mall. It turned out to be a fateful event because I ran into another employee who'd been fired from the rail yard the Christmas before. She was now running a security team at this large urban mall.

Before the rail job I'd actually done my security training and had my license. I wasn't able to get hired at that time because I had no experience. The people that trained me failed to mention that. It's an old scam. Schools of security people paying up to $400 a pop to get licensed with zero prospect of employment. The company ran their own security company as a sideline – the schooling and scamming of hopeful guards was where the big money was. But I digress.

I never got to use my license. I was handed the rail gig in February 2013 by a friend and at that point I'd been gainfully unemployed for 3 years so I jumped on it without hesitation. How hard could inspecting cars be? Famous last words.

My associate at the mall had no positions open for me or I would have been hired right there. Instead, she suggested another security company not far from my home. How fortuitous.

I drove immediately to their office and filled out the application form. The secretary told me I'd be contacted within 24 hours if everything checked out. True enough, I was asked to come in for an interview that Friday.

I was greeted by the Human Resources officer and after looking me up and down said, "You will have to cut your hair!"

"No problem," I said.

"I have a condominium in the city that needs a night guard but I'm wondering if you might be right for something else I have in mind."

"What's that?" I said.

She responded with a question, "How do you feel about cemeteries?"

"I'm not superstitious about them if that's what you mean. My wife and I visit cemeteries as a hobby. We took ghost tours in New Orleans on our Honeymoon. I'm good with it."

I didn't have time to tell her more. I kept the answer simple, but the explanation would have meant regaling her with my entire life story relating to death. But I can talk about it here.

STARING INTO THE FACE OF DEATH

Looking back over my 50-plus years it may seem like I've led a rather charmed life. Not rich and not immensely successful but given opportunities and experiences most people don't get in ten lifetimes. Much of it was afforded me through hard work and networking and having a large family to see that I was looked after while growing up. I was the only male child on my Dad's side of the family so I was often spoiled more times than not. I never took it for granted. Many of my friends never had the same luxury.

What my family couldn't do was protect me from death. It was the yang to my charmed ying. I was a pretty happy kid with a very dark cloud of sadness hiding in my psychic closet. Having escaped near death at a very early age – I was born with blood clots in my head and was hospitalized for the better part of my second year on earth – I found myself very sensitive to outside stimulus especially when people were angry at me. I cried a lot as a kid and as a male child of the 1960s that was wholly unacceptable. I bottled it up.

But the sadness would be unleashed each time a family member died. It was frequent and it was devastating for a kid. These people were supposed to protect me from the Boogieman. I lost a cousin to leukemia at age 11. My Dad's sister-in-law and my step-grandfather in succession after that; As a teenager it was my great grandmother then my grandfather on my Mom's side then it seemed to be a litany of great aunts and great uncles followed by the biggest blow when I was 27 – my Dad's mother – which sent me into a personal spiral culminating in the collapse of my first marriage.

She had been a guiding force in my life. She drove me across Canada when I was 12 and showed me there was a great big beautiful world out there ready to explore. She instilled the wanderlust in me to carry on with my own adventures like that one she took me on in 1975 and those adventures ultimately led to poking around in cemeteries.

My wife shares the same interest I do in history and Gothic ruins. She also loves watching ghost stories on TV. Cemeteries are the easiest to investigate and we've jumped at any chance to plod through them. Our honeymoon found us in New Orleans wandering through St. Louis

Cemetery #1. We would also go to the resting place of the Salem witches in Massachusetts and on another trip we hit three cemeteries in Los Angeles to see the final resting place of some of movie and TV's greatest stars.

To some, it's a ghoulish hobby. We've never given it a second thought. Cemeteries are archaeology without the digging. I've applied the same logic to tracking down and documenting my family's genealogy going back 400 years to England. Apparently, there's a church graveyard in Chapel-En-Le-Frith littered with Vernons. I hope one day to return there and pay my respects.

With the security job mine I was about to come full circle as my most recent ancestors are buried in the cemeteries I was about to patrol full-time as a Cemetery Cop.

CHAPTER TWO

IN SECURITY

Learning how to secure a cemetery seemed like an easy task on the surface. How hard could it be? You lock/unlock a few gates, you secure a few buildings and doors, you make sure no one's locked inside the grounds and you go home.

My orientation took two days. Beacon Hill Cemetery was the biggest municipal gravesite in the province. 12 square kilometres covering four major arterial roads – two of which sliced the cemetery into three sections. 51 separate gates, 17 buildings, and half a million dead souls counting on one person every day to make sure the place was left the way it was found albeit with a few more tenants.

You didn't just walk around and fiddle with gates and doors. It was a military operation on a strict timetable to accommodate staff and visitors. And those timetables shifted based on the seasons. The opening of the cemetery stayed the same, but in the summer months the facility remained open past sundown and in the winter it closed at dinnertime. Signs are posted at every entrance denoting this. Every straggler, every shut-in, and every person with suspicious motives, without fail, would claim they had no idea when the cemetery closed. I never believed any of them for a minute. These were locals and the cemetery had been there over 100 years. If you lived next door to a graveyard I would expect you to know its hours of operation especially if there was a chance of getting locked inside of it. But we'll get to those people soon enough.

The orientation and training was split into a morning shift on Day One and an evening shift on Day Two. Seven hours and eight hours respectively. The guard training me was nice enough to not ram everything down my throat in one day because a regular shift is 15 hours straight with only two meal breaks. I was thankful for that. It allowed me to take notes. I filled 20 pages of a three-ringed binder and with good reason. The tasks for the guards required a degree in critical thinking and time management.

You had to have all the perimeter gates in the cemetery open so that the public could access the grounds before 7AM. That would include cyclists, joggers, dog walkers and people just trying to bisect the neighbourhood to get to transit or somewhere else for their jobs or appointments. In the early days of my watch I was arriving at 6AM just so I could refer to my notes and have time to think through the next steps.

But it meant getting up at 4:45 AM in the morning, heading to the security office, picking up my patrol car, my itinerary work kit, my radio, and my site keys and then battling traffic for nearly an hour usually in the dark. You just prayed there were no traffic accidents, construction hold ups or weather issues heading there because if you were late, the locals would complain to the cemetery bosses that security had not opened up time. Thankfully, it only happened once to me. As time went on I got faster opening and many of the grounds keepers who liked me and arrived when I did would open various gates on my behalf saving me valuable time in getting my first round of patrols done.

As I said, there were 51 gates and the distance between the nearest and the farthest gate was about three kilometres as the crow flies. But in a car you can't fly like a crow because the cemetery also contained 32 kilometres of roadway none of which lead directly from the back of the cemetery to the front. Most were winding, many dead ended, and none of them were lit except where they were intersected by the major roads or led to a public building like an office, a mausoleum or the Visitation Centre. Luckily, the patrol car was equipped with a powerful spotlight on the roof that could spin 270 degrees. It would save my life on more than one occasion.

The front gate on Beacon Hill Road had to be opened first. It contained a lock box embedded in it with the keys to the cemetery. I had the key to the lock box. I can proudly say I never forgot it after leaving the security office in the morning. But, other guards did. At least one guard lost the key in a snow bank one night in the dark when locking up. That didn't go well for him.

I did three 15 hours shifts in a row, normally. The other four days of the week were divvied up between two other guards. The gent who trained me had health issues and didn't work too many days in a row. But Billy was the best at what he did. I'm grateful to have had him as my teacher. He told me all the difficult parts of the job including what fussy staff members to tap-dance around and how to speed up patrols and fill out reports.

"Stay inconspicuous but make sure you're visible when you need to be. The staff needs to know when they can call on you and the public needs to be reassured that there's someone nearby if they run into trouble. In other words, stay out of the fucking way until you're called on. Pick sniper points in the cemetery and don't stay too long or they'll think you're having a nap. The grounds guys are your eyes. They'll let you know if they see anything suspicious. Buy them coffee and they'll be your friends for life."

It sounded impossible. I was one guard in one car who had to be everywhere at once. How the hell was I going to do everything I needed to do every day and then reverse it all again at night for lock up? I couldn't bend space and time or at least that's what I thought on that first day of training.

At 6AM the cemetery is completely empty until the gates are open. That allowed me to drive at top speed. In this case that meant about 40 km/h amongst the graves and monuments where I would then jump out like a pizza delivery man and run to each gate where a master key would undo a padlock and then the wrought-iron gate could be pushed or pulled into position, and tied off. Then it was onto the next one. The order in which the gates were opened would determine how quickly it could be done. It took months of trial and error to get it down to an art form. Billy had his way of doing it, I tweaked and revised it my own liking.

Not all the gates were near roads. Many times the car had to be parked and a small jog down a pathway led to the gate. You literally jogged because time was of the essence. In the winter those pathways were covered in snow, sometimes a foot deep. In the spring they were covered in mud. Billy showed me which of these pathways was wide enough to handle the patrol car. They were fairly flat access points and no gravestones were close by so there was no risk of damage. This would prove problematic on more than a few occasions but I'll get to that later.

Oh, and did I mention I had to unlock and kill the security alarms on a number of buildings at the same time? So the morning exercise was really a series of gate, gate, door, gate, door, gate, gate, door, door, door, gate, etc. And if you got to a door and the alarm had been tripped, or God forbid, had failed to be set the night before by the previous guard or a cleaning crew it was mayhem. Reports, phone calls and all kinds of awkward conversations would result – ones you didn't want to have with either the security company higher ups or the cemetery bosses because they'd inevitably blame you even if it wasn't.

Every alarm on every building had a different security code. You think you have trouble remembering people's phone numbers? 17 buildings, 17 codes. You had to memorize them all and if you input a wrong number the system would lock down and a call to the alarm company was in order and a report would have to be filled out with a possible reprimand from security headquarters. I found clever ways of keeping track of the numbers including writing them all on my arm before the day started. It's one of the reasons we wore long sleeved shirts as part of our uniforms – even in the 35C heat. Eventually I remembered the codes after months of repetition.

Following the opening of the gates and buildings I did a drive through of the entire grounds because the sun was now up and I could see what kind of movement there was on site. Aside from the joggers and dog walkers and cyclists there were also kids walking through to school and stay-at-home moms pushing strollers. There were activity clubs of seniors doing power walks, site-seeing groups taking in the Gothic history of the graves and the dozens of maintenance teams mowing, trimming, gardening, watering and digging.

The full-time grounds keepers were grave diggers and maintenance staff whose sole job it was to keep on top of funeral services. They dug graves a day ahead and sometimes two days ahead if there was a large number of interments on any given day. The most I recall on a single day was 23 events. These guys were in at 6.30AM and out at 3PM. On the busy days they'd be there until 5PM.

The seasonal staff consisted mostly of students whose job it was to cut the grass, plant flowers and bushes, clear dead branches and leaves and change the seventy-five 40 gallon oil-drum garbage cans placed all over the cemetery. To everyone's credit, there was rarely a piece of litter anywhere on site unless it blew there from an adjoining street. Ironically, you could get visitors to observe the litter ordinance, but you couldn't keep them or their dogs from pissing or shitting on graves. I'm only half kidding about the people.

Long before I began working at Beacon Hill there was an incident of human defecation on the grave of the family of a famous musician. Someone returned to the gravesite often and took a shit on it. The person was eventually apprehended, arrested and charged with any number of infractions not the least of which was public indecency.

I once caught a woman relieving herself behind a tree in front of the Visitation Centre after it had closed one day. I saw her check the doors to the building and once she realized she couldn't get in she disappeared behind a pine tree nearby.

I slowly rolled up to the edge of the road nearest the tree and shouted, "I can see you!"

She peaked out from behind the tree. She was leaning forward and trying do her pants back up and talk to me at the same time.

"I'm just visiting a relative."

"Really? Who would that be?"

She panicked and ran passed me and back out the front gate as quickly as she could. It was kind of ridiculous, really, because there were electric portal toilets located near every major entrance. She had to pass one to enter the cemetery!

JAIMIE VERNON

THE GRASS MENAGERIE

And then there were the animals, a lot of animals. Squirrels, chipmunks, ground hogs, a hundred varieties of bird including red-tail hawks, mice, rats, bats, possum, skunk, deer, cats and even coy-wolves who would wander up from the ravine below the valley section of the cemetery. The raccoons. Massive, dog-sized raccoons. By the end of my tenure there I had counted 33 families of raccoon with a minimum of two adults and three kids in each pack. They became landmarks for when I was patrolling in the dark and entertainment on slow nights while I was eating dinner. The cemetery was an artificial but highly functioning eco-system and the goal was to allow the dead to become part of that cycle of growth and renewal.

The first deer I saw was walking along the ridge of the valley that led into the ravine. I caught a glimpse as I was doing a foot patrol behind the family crypts that dotted the hill checking for remnants of garbage left behind by people who regularly sneaked in to party behind the crypts. I reached down to pick up some empty beer cans and caught movement from my peripheral. I stood up slowly and two crypts away was an adult doe frozen in its tracks with only its ears and nose in motion. I walked slowly toward it and snapped a picture on my phone. It ran down the ridge into the valley below.

My second encounter was a little more interactive. After locking up the pedestrian gate in Section 3 one night I was driving a fair clip (well, as fair as you could go on a dark cemetery road through a forest) and there was a shadow that obscured the light coming in my driver window. I looked to my left and there at my eye level was a giant eyeball and ear from a deer that was racing beside me. Had I rolled down my window I could have rubbed its nose.

I slammed on the brakes, my heart pounding in my chest and the deer – which was an adult buck – cut across the front of my car and disappeared into an ash scattering area to my right. I waited for it to come back out, but it disappeared. Over the next year I'd see more deer hovering around the ravine area as they were coming up from the valley mostly out of curiosity and to nibble on berries and flowers all around fences near the perimeter of the cemetery.

NEVER CRY COY-WOLF

More alarming was the frequent sighting of coy-wolf tracks on freshly fallen snow. I was familiar with them as I'd had some rather close calls at the rail yard where I once worked. That work site also had a ravine and the coy-wolves often used it to cross the rail yard to parts unknown.

One night after a rather sizeable snows fall over the course of an entire week my access to the gates in the ravine was seriously obstructed. It would mean crawling over a snow bank at the foot of the path leading down to the ravine. I parked my patrol car at the end of the cul-de-sac leading to the path with the car's spotlight aimed at the snow bank; I then prepared myself for the adventure by grabbing a flashlight from my knapsack, my walkie-talkie and some lock de-icer in case the padlock on the gate had frozen during the day and stepped out of the car.

I turned to look over at the snow bank before shutting the car door and there, sitting on the very top and staring eye-level to me was a coy-wolf. The ones I'd ever seen close up were generally scrawny and covered in mange. This one appeared quite healthy and was surveying its surroundings. I opened the car door slowly and stood with one foot in and one foot out of the vehicle and peered at the animal from a safe distance across the hood of the car.

I expect that he couldn't see me because the spotlight was aimed directly at him. It was more than blinding to anyone caught in the beam. The air was brisk with no wind so I'm not sure whether it could smell me or not. The only sound was the din of my car radio. I reached in and turned it off. I stood up again to take another look and the coy-wolf was now facing the opposite direction. I could hear it panting and then stopping to sniff the air. It was like a scene from *'The Good, The Bad and The Ugly.'* I was Lee Van Cleef, the coy-wolf was Clint Eastwood. I wasn't going to win this thing.

I got back in the patrol car and waited except now from my sitting position my vantage point my view was obstructed. I could only see the coy-wolf's legs. I waited ten minutes and he didn't seem to budge. It was then that I realized that locking the ravine gate that night was a low priority. The path was filled with snow. It was also filled with coy-wolf and maybe more than on. Anyone dumb enough to try and break into the cemetery from that entrance was taking their life into their hands.

I slowly drove away and watched the coy-wolf disappear down the back side of the snow bank in my rear view mirror. Clearly we'd both had enough. I never saw the animal again and I'd convinced the cemetery to allow me to keep the gate locked until such time as the snow receded and access could be achieved at a later date via the patrol car if necessary.

CATS ON A HOT TIN CHERRY PICKER

One of the many maintenance buildings had its own mouser, a cat named Buster. He was a stray that wandered into the cemetery one day and never left. One of the security guards began feeding him long before I started the job and sometimes when I picked up my patrol car at the start of a shift there'd be a box of canned food that needed to be delivered to that maintenance building. Buster appreciated the wet food as the cemetery's maintenance guys only fed him dry food if they remembered to feed him at all. He'd always greet me at the farthest of the garage doors as I began my process of closing up the building. He'd walk with me as I closed them one by one because he knew at the end of the routine he'd get fed.

There were also many single cats that wandered in and out of the property but I expect they were on alert to the raccoons already laying claim to the territory and would run back home to their pampered suburban lives. The exception was the mausoleum that was under construction. In an alleyway behind the building were the work machines and materials that were left securely there each night by the contractors. The neighbourhood cats congregated on a small retaining wall that separated the alleyway from the perimeter fence. I'd have to secure the back door leading from the alley into the building and would often step outside to see the cats.

On any given day there could 10 of them all in various states of feral prickliness. Some were quite curious and would immediately come to me looking for food while the others remained on the retaining wall or the large two-storey cherry picker that was used to lift drywall and marble slabs. These cats were at eye level to me and usually just sat in an aloof sprawl disinterested in my presence. I never fed any of them and always wore gloves while I was back there. It seemed unwise to allow any of them to bite or scratch me. They were friendly enough, but I had no interest in being there should a fight break out.

RACCOON CITY

By far the raccoons were the biggest pains in the ass especially in the spring when the babies showed up. Parental raccoons are ten times more vicious than your everyday garbage snagging scavenger raccoons. They're angry and protective.

Imagine my surprise then when closing the cemetery one night and I came across three blind baby raccoons sitting directly in the centre of one of the access roads. I was on my way toward one of the main entrances when I stopped the car to try and get them off the road. A cyclist saw what I was doing and came to help.

We weren't sure whether touching the animals was a good idea only because a kamikaze parental unit could have caused some serious damage to either one of us if we attempted to do so. The idea was to push them along with a piece of cardboard and the front wheel of the bike. It took nearly 30 minutes to get the three of them to crawl in the same direction and onto the grass. There was some serious cuteness going on there, but where the hell was the mother raccoon?

I returned to the spot after the cemetery had been secured that night and found them in the grass with about a dozen other raccoons foraging for food. It was the endless circle for them. Eat, sleep, breed, and harass the humans. Every night it was the same. I'd end up watching these truck-sized animals jumping in and out of 40 gallon oil drum waste receptacles throughout the cemetery as they attempted to extract the day's discarded food brought in by visitors.

They're not much to worry about in ones or twos, but on one particular evening I had just left my daily report on the cemetery manager's desk at head office and was returning to my patrol car so I could head off site. I looked over at the front gate where I'd have to exit and saw a long jagged silhouette against the bottom of the front gates and it was moving.

I got in my car, hit the spotlight and drove toward the gate. The light caught the glowing eyes of about 15 raccoons all milling about at the front entrance. That was problematic. I needed to get out, open the gate, drive the car through, get out and close the gate behind me to secure the cemetery. They were blocking my access.

I was prepared. I never threw my lunch or dinner wrappings away each day. I always took them with me and disposed of my messes off site. Tonight the raccoons were in for a treat. I had a half-eaten burger and some fries in a bag. I pulled up to the gates where the animals seemed quite disinterested in moving and opened my driver's window. I removed the food from the bag and threw each item onto the grass as far as I could away from the gates. Every last one of them ran after the food.

I drove the last few feet to the gate and jumped out. The noise of the animals fighting over the food was unsettling. I threw open the gate, ran back to the car and got in. I coasted through the gateway and got back out. As I walked back to close the gates behind me the raccoons looked up and some of them started to head toward me zombie-like. It was like Night of the Barely Fed. I slammed the gates shut and stuck the padlock on. They were now inches from me – many of them standing on their hind legs trying to negotiate an exit strategy. Had they been smaller they could have crawled underneath but luckily they were all exceptionally large and locked inside for the night. In the morning they'd all be gone again except for piles of bandit poop.

CHAPTER THREE

CHECK. CHECK. ONE. TWO

Following the early morning opening of the gates and buildings at Beacon Hill Cemetery and an initial inspection of the grounds once the sun came up, it was time to check in. We had to call our dispatcher at the security office every hour. The time itself didn't matter as long as we were consistent and called on the hour thereafter.

Occasionally they'd spot check you – especially if the dispatcher changed shifts and a new guy came on. He or she would need to confirm who was still in the field at the various sites – condos, shopping malls, shipping facilities, rail yards, and the cemetery. I rarely missed my calls because if they checked on you twice and you didn't answer there'd be a supervisor dispatched to the site to find out if you had your radio off, you were sleeping or, worse, you were dead. That latter happened at least once that I know of. An officer missed two spot checks on the radio and when the mobile crew went to see what was going on they found him dead beside his patrol car. Heart attack.

The next point of business was to inform the cemetery staff that security was on-site. Head office was near the Beacon Hill front gates and it was home base for the administrators who dealt with staff issues and funeral arrangements – either through third party funeral homes or in-house where full-service funerals/interments could be facilitated. Those services included catering, church services and mourners all in the Visitation Centre.

The receptionist, Emily, knew all. She was the link between the admin staff and what was going on in the field each day. I would grab a fresh visitor map from her desk and she'd rhyme off the itinerary for that day. She'd give me the event time and name of the deceased and what section of the cemetery they were being interred or having their ashes scattered. From there it allowed me to plot out traffic needs. Was it strictly graveside? Would there be a contingent of mourners at the Visitation Centre? Was it a big service? A small private memorial? I'd spend a good 20 minutes plotting it out and making notes.

From there I'd move down to the Visitation Centre itself to confirm what they were doing that day in the building and the timing of access and egress and to co-ordinate with their funeral assistants on traffic control. Lots of traffic control. There was many access points to the Visitation Centre parking lot so it was important people could park confidently and that they could actually find the VC in the first place. It often meant sniping a spot near the front gate and directing cars to where they needed to go. Though the cemetery was clearly marked with signage and colour-specific painted lines to guide you to various buildings, sometimes it was just easier to hand them a map with little arrows drawn on it to guide them. 1 out of every 10 visitors still got lost and would end up right back where I was standing.

WHITE LINE FEVER

One such visitor and her husband spent 30 minutes trying to find a burial service they were late for. They'd asked ground crew where the spot was. The answer was to follow the painted line white line in one direction or the other. The woman from this couple had had enough. They pulled up beside me while I was sitting near a gate in my patrol car.

"We cannot find the plot where this service is taking place and now we're late because the roads in here are ridiculous."

She showed me the map she had been given and I pointed at the ground beside my patrol car and said, "This line will take you exactly to where you want to go."

It was as if I'd murdered her children. She started screaming at the top of her lungs, "I'M NOT FOLLOWING ANY MORE LINES!!!" The tirade continued, "YOU ARE GOING TO DRIVE US WHERE WE NEED TO GO AND YOU'RE GOING TO DO IT…NOW!!!"

Her husband was out of the car at this point because she'd started to cry. She was standing on the white line on the road and was stomping her feet like an impetuous child, "SOMEONE BETTER FIX THIS. I DEMAND IT!! I DEMAND IT!!!"

The husband was mortified. He came over to me and leaned into my window, "Can you please help us?"

Normally, I would have continued my conversation with this woman and helped immediately. Uncharacteristically, I talked to her husband instead, as he was the poor soul that had to deal with this woman on a daily basis. It wasn't hard to see that this wasn't just because of the stress of a funeral, but that she was a privileged, spoiled human being used to getting her own way.

"I'm within my rights to have both of you kicked out of here for that kind of behaviour. Look...traffic is backing up behind your car. Tell your wife to dial it down and get back in the car and you can follow me to the gravesite. If she carries on I'll have her removed."

He apologized for her and grabbed her by the elbow and escorted her back to the car. I did a U-turn in front of them and had them follow me. We drove along the white line down a hill. The line turned right at the bottom. They followed me closely. Immediately, I pulled over behind a hearse. They pulled over behind me.

I got out and tapped on the driver's window. The husband rolled it down and I crouched so that I was eye level with him and his passenger. I said sarcastically, "You're here. Follow the white God damned line backwards when you want to leave."

THE INTERRED

Between services I was still expected to patrol the rest of the cemetery with eyes on the ground looking for the hopeless, the helpless or the reckless. At times I was thankful that the cemetery was as big as it was. It allowed for slow drives from section to section. It gave me pause to get out of the car and walk. I was determined not put all the weight back on that I'd lost doing my rail yard job during the previous two years. It would turn out to be a losing battle because in a 15-hour day the most you could really walk around was a few hours in total. You couldn't be too far away from your vehicle in case you were needed on the other side of the cemetery.

In those times when the weather was good I could walk through each section of the graveyard – studying history, making mental notes of surnames and trying to piece together in my mind's eye the life story of these lost souls. It was sobering. Looking at the mortality rates of generations gone by. So many died young. Many plots contained five or even six generations of one family or there'd be adjoining graves of relatives. There were also the rich, the famous and the notorious. Politicians, sports figures, military figures going as far back as the Rebellion, musicians, artists, TV and movie personalities, inventors, doctors, lawyers, captains of industry and the victims of great disasters like ship sinkings, airplane crashes, and murders. Death made no distinction. Everyone was under the same tree covered canopy. This wasn't just a self-indulgent exercise, either because I would also make note of broken or defaced gravestones, graffiti and even suspicious items placed on graves.

Usually people placed food, pebbles, coins or other mementos on top or beside the graves. Sometimes they placed adult diapers. Yes. On one occasion someone had run through the cemetery placing adult diapers on headstones. The staff and myself were quick to clear them out before the public noticed. When it happens once you write it off as a prank. When it happens three times you get alarmed that there's a disturbed individual in the cemetery. Neither myself, the other security guards or the staff ever caught the person. It stopped as quickly as it had begun.

I also did perimeter checks of the buildings themselves, specifically the five mausoleums on site. They varied from the very old and Gothic to the most recent one that was under construction the entire time I worked there and housed the feral cats. Despite the cemetery being ecumenical, three of the mausoleums were geared specifically to Christians – almost exclusively to Italians, Portuguese and Greeks. The ethnic and religious communities in our city paid to have them built and maintained on their behalf. They were ornate and ostentatious. The bodies would be placed in crypts in the walls and family members would decorate the marble faceplate with photos and religious iconography and letters and cards written to the deceased from family members. The heartbreak was that these heartfelt pieces of correspondence were almost always from children or grandchildren. The mausoleum was a living document of the grieving. The mausoleums were also emblazoned in marble, gold leaf and life-sized creepy-as-shit statues of various figures from the Bible. If you didn't focus during foot patrols occasionally you'd turn a corner and Jesus himself would scare the Jesus out of you.

Tucked away in the corners of each mausoleum was the newest idea that the funeral industry was incorporating – urn cabinets and display windows for the cremated. It's one thing to walk down hallways of plaques with names on them with bodies safely encased in the very walls of the buildings but I always found it unsettling to look directly at rows of people's ashes like so many curio cabinets.

"Oh, look, here's Uncle Gustav's ashes in a wooden cigar box surrounded by his favourite things – scratch lottery tickets, a photo of his pre-deceased wife, and a dog whistle." Was the dog in there with him too? I felt like a voyeur. You couldn't help it. Like the gravestones outside, every cubic foot window contained a story either glorious or tragic, sometimes simultaneously. The most poignant I ever saw was that of a Czech freedom fighter from the Second World War whose modestly decorated urn was accompanied by his war medals, his citizenship card to Canada and photos of him with his grandchildren. He died at 92. It was a great life by the looks of it.

GOING GOTH

The single Gothic mausoleum, however, is a horror film personified as it had been built over 100 years ago. It was an elegant and classical design with tapestry carpets, vaulted ceilings and marble walls and pillars imported from Europe that came over on ships that may or may not have made it safely across the Atlantic. It contains a chapel upstairs as the centerpiece of the building with crystal chandeliers that sparkle from the sun pouring in through vaulted transom windows overhead. The magnates of industry and wealth are interred here. It features 1,000 families who preferred their crypt to be indoors and not out on the grounds in the insufferable weather. Every marble panel is hand engraved with the names and important dates of each person inside the walls. And in the summer those walls sweat like a steam bath. The ongoing decay, even 100 years later, was evident just entering the building. The smell would linger on your clothes. Roses and lavender are said to cover the smell. They do not.

Those rich enough to have tombs built inside the mausoleum occupy the back walls of the building. Up to a dozen bodies with a stained glass window as a gift of natural light and a bronze gated door to keep the riff raff out; that included us security guards because only the cemetery staff had keys to these crypts. Some of them even contain the furniture and other possessions of the deceased. One such tomb looked like a studio apartment for a student who would never return.

Downstairs was more modern as the cemetery had dug out the basement for a section of more contemporary interments that could be accessed through glass doors and stairways leading out to the front of the building. There are also back hallways with narrow maintenance stairwells that lead to the parking lot for the mausoleum staff and people accessing the maintenance building next door.

The smell of death was even stronger here. So much so that the cemetery kept industrial strength dehumidifiers running 24 hours a day to keep the sweat off the walls and lingering scent to a minimum. I never got used to it.

This was done for practical reasons as well: pests. Dead bodies decompose and attract a variety of insects not the least of is the death beetles which are about the size of a poppy seed. And they're creepy as hell when they congregate, en masse, on the nameplate of a crypt or between the spaces in the walls. The cemetery had a team of pest control guys in every week managing the ongoing invasion. It would never be eliminated, but it needed to be managed if for no other reason than not having a loved one come in and see swarms of these things crawling all over a crypt. It was also unsettling to see them when the lights were off and I was patrolling with nothing but a flashlight after hours.

Flowers, both real and artificial, decorated every corner of the mausoleums. The real ones would nearly masque the other odours, but I always found that the sickly sweet smell of roses was synonymous with death mainly because funeral ceremonies were generally filled with truck loads of them in baskets and wreaths.

The most common accoutrements in the mausoleums were tall, eight-inch praying candles. They generally came in two colours – opaque candy-apple red with a tapered opening or a white glazed surface featuring a religious picture emblazoned on the side with a fluted opening. People would use long tinder sticks to set off the wicks, pray to their deity and their loved one and then leave the candles behind – still lit – when they left.

It was a fire hazard. Signs on every building warn people not to light candles inside the buildings. Few people obeyed the rule. On more than one occasion small smoldering fires had begun from candles left unattended. The mausoleums were generally drafty and with windows left open to vent the noxious gases – especially in the heat of summer temperatures – candles would easily tip over. The mausoleum carpets were supposed to be fire retardant but we never wanted to test the theory. Frequent patrols inside the buildings were conducted for no other reason than to ensure all the candles had been extinguished.

Following several visits from family members the candles would have no wax left to burn and they'd be tossed in the garbage cans around the cemetery and replaced immediately with an identical new candle. The ritual would continue ad infinitum.

What was not tolerated at all was food in the mausoleums. Unlike outdoors where food would generally be scavenged by the animals, food in the mausoleum generated more pests. Similarly, any real flowers put in the mausoleums as their life expectancy was quite short and it was a constant struggle for staff to keep on top of removing them before they became unsightly, rotting piles on the floor and walls. It wasn't unusual to see a stack of baskets and wreaths three or four feet high outside the front doors of the mausoleums waiting to be picked up by maintenance staff for disposal. Such was the cycle of death.

CHAPTER FOUR

WHAT PRICE DEATH?

At first glance the grounds at the cemetery – or any cemetery, really – seems like a mini-city. The headstones rise from the ground like apartment towers. Though the Greeks didn't create the term, two compound Greek words inform it: necropolis also known as City of the Dead. It's how Europeans described the landscape of graveyards at the turn of the 19th century. The more sensitive modern term is resting place. You wouldn't know it from the activity at Beacon Hill.

As with the mausoleums, the graves themselves have become reflections of the world of the living. Flowers, wreaths, toys, balloons, food and every manner of topiary you could imagine. It's hard to tell sometimes where the focus on the deceased actually is in the equation. Some of the graves resemble garish and gaudy concrete gardens filled with lanterns, bird feeders, cement cherubs and angels and other religious iconography. It drives the maintenance staff nuts because they're responsible for mowing the grass and more times than not end up running over errant or misplaced lawn ornaments. The complaints from the families of the deceased are endless. They firmly believe the damage is deliberate. The truth is that the damage is often unavoidable. The compromise is families who do their own landscaping or bring in professional companies to do it for them. It has become an industry unto itself.

It's a study in contrasts too. Not just by culture or religion, but by era. The historically Gothic grave marker made of limestone or granite etched with English script and chiseled serif fonts has given way to foot stones which designate individual members of a family plot or where there are tight grave formations. The other is machine-polished marble headstones so reflective as to radiate sunlight off them on extremely bright sunny days. In lieu of true material wealth, even the poorest of souls can rest eternally in a plot that looks like the front cover of an issue of *Better Homes & Gardens*.

With cemetery land being at a premium now the administrators are looking for new ways to generate revenue. The misconception is that it's a scam. Funerals are not cheap even if you want to stick someone in a plywood box. The reason costs can't be capped actually has to do with families in need of eternal care for their loved ones. That includes the mowing of the grass and possibly planting of flowers in the summer or having a wreath placed on the grave by staff at Christmas time for a minimum of 99 years. Those costs rise every year but the families pay for the procedure only once – at the time of interment. You can see the dilemma. People who were buried 75 or 100 years ago are still receiving personal care.

That means the newest burials are subsidizing all those pre-existing graves. And as land runs out who is going to pay for all that upkeep on half-a-million graves in 30 or 40 years? It's a conundrum that all cemeteries are now finding themselves in.

I went to visit another graveyard in the city where some of my very distant relatives were buried in an effort to put names and dates into my ongoing genealogy research. This graveyard was very old and these relatives had died in the early 20th century. The info on them was still contained on index cards. The staff was able to locate the document rather quickly and it indicated that the eternal care had expired. There was an amount owing of $60 to continue the service. They asked me if I wanted to step up. As I was only remotely related I found it hard to justify. The grave, which didn't have a headstone at all, would eventually grow over and be forgotten. The deceased would still occupy the space forever whether I had them mow the grass or not. And this cemetery was nearly full. One day not long from now they will run into financial problems. I certainly hope the funeral industry figures out a way of sustaining itself, as land continues to become scarce.

The Americans have the same issues and have introduced the unsavory idea of grave renting. That is, the deceased is interred in a plot for X number of years before they're exhumed, put in a mass grave, and the single plot is resold to a current family in need; it's capitalism at its heartless, pragmatic worst. Canada has not stooped to such a tactic. Instead, they're innovating. Many plots are bought decades in advance for entire families. As we've seen in census studies modern families are no longer as big as they once were. Many are selling their extra, unused, plots back to the cemeteries.

Meanwhile, the most common and accepted way is cremation. There has been a cultural shift to less organic funerals and a bigger push toward either keeping the ashes indefinitely in the family home or interring the ashes in mausoleums or having them scattered. Ashes to ashes...

Beacon Hill has a forested area dedicated to memorial scatterings for loved ones. Technically you can scatter human ashes anywhere, but many prefer the peace of mind of doing it in a cemetery without the formality of a graveside event. Markers and plaques are erected in the wooded area as a memoriam. These areas are beautifully landscaped with unobtrusive stones paths, wood chips, wind chimes and even pastoral music piped into the area through hidden speakers buried beneath the floor of the forest.

The maintenance staff is incredible at their jobs and to make visitors feel they are in a natural rather than man-made setting. With the historic tree base already in place the hills and valley and existing contours of the property lend themselves to nature's beauty among the clatter of the city surrounding it. It's a green oasis of sorts and it invites misuse of the area by those who mistake the cemetery for run-of-the-mill parkland.

Cyclists were sometimes a hazard by virtue of their speed and, just once, by their nakedness. I was alerted to a guy wandering around the cemetery on a bicycle in his birthday suit. He was decidedly trunk and didn't put up with much of a fight. He didn't seem too concerned about people seeing him in the all together, but the people had a problem with it. He was escorted painlessly off the site.

Joggers were the same. Fortunately, there were no disrobing women, but there were disrobing men. Teams of guys in fitness clubs would do timed runs through the kilometres of roadways and many were in Speedos or the workout wardrobe equivalent. These outfits were barely acceptable beachwear, never mind cemetery wear. I begged management to post signs but they never did so it was up to me to police the grounds looking for what my Granny used to call 'mashers'.

I'm reminded of an incident where a woman was visiting her mother's grave and beside it was a man visiting his mother's grave at the same time. It was a warm and sunny day so the man felt compelled to not only picnic on the plot – but remove most of his clothes. He wasn't quite naked, but it was very inappropriate. The woman visiting her mother was incensed. She tracked me down to file a complaint. I went by the plot and told the guy that he was more than free to visit his mother, but disrobing would not be tolerated. He told me to piss off and continued his sunbathing. I was technically powerless to do anything except file a formal complaint on the woman's behalf and note the plot number to the cemetery staff.

Some belief systems have mourners sit for hours beside the graves to pray or contemplate. The first known lawn furniture was loveseats made of wrought-iron that were designed in New Orleans for those who wanted to lounge with the dearly departed. That tradition was eventually adapted into a mundane work-a-day design for people sitting in their own backyards, but the origin began in cemeteries not unlike Beacon Hill.

There are benches and loveseats and entire stoops wrapped around some of the biggest and oldest trees in the facility. There are no picnic tables despite requests from visitors. Eating there is not encouraged especially as it attracts animals. Again, the cemetery is not a park despite how it might look.

We had a long game of hide and seek with one regular in the cemetery who insisted on randomly placing fresh apples atop tombstones. No one could get a handle on who it was but we began to get complaints because the food was rotting and spoiling on the headstones causing stains on the shiny polished surfaces. It was never an issue until one particular family member found that it was happening on her husband's tombstone once a week. She wanted the culprit caught. She demanded a full investigation. As much as I don't blame her for not wanting the grave defaced, her outrageous reaction was over-stated. The apple was usually picked clean by the animals in the cemetery leaving nothing but the peel. The stains washed away by frequent rain.

Eventually we found who was doing it. It was a very nice older Chinese fellow who walked the entire cemetery every morning on his way to visiting relatives in the Gothic mausoleum. No one would have suspected. He dressed in a loose-fitting Berber overcoat with flowing black work pants. And he carried a satchel. I always assumed it was candles and whatever he needed to honour the relatives he was visiting in the mausoleum. Turns out it was full of apples. Ironically, he never placed an apple in the mausoleum. We told him that he was very generous in honouring others in the cemetery but the families of these people had asked that he stop. He didn't understand exactly, but the apple offerings stopped right after that.

LOCATION, LOCATION, LOCATION!

As someone once said to me in passing, "It would be the most idyllic setting in the world if not for the dead people."

It sounds aloof. It sounds disrespectful but there's a dark, sardonic edge to working among those who can no longer speak for themselves. It makes you question everything about the universe. Why are we here? Why do we die? And why do we keep our dead in tiny cities and build fences around them to keep them locked inside for all eternity?

It's hard to imagine what the world would look like if all the cemeteries that ever existed were still where they were originally built and all the bodies remained.

To that end Beacon Hill is an amalgam of four or five historic cemeteries. Many were moved from other locations as the urban sprawl encroached and development land, rather than the dead, became the biggest commodity. Beacon Hill became a collection box for the city's former citizens. And who knows how many bodies were actually left in those locations when the construction equipment moved in to over-turn the soil and drive re-bar into the ground.

It plays out in your mind's eye like that scene from the movie Poltergeist. It's not a stretch to believe that headstones were relocated while the bodies from those graves failed to come along with them. I feel badly for the ancestors who may be looking for the final destinations of their great-great-great relations. Their names are on headstones in Beacon Hill but no one can confirm if the people are actually buried there or not. Plaques do indicate that this might be the case.

Like all cemeteries Beacon Hill also has a Field of Lost Souls. It is here that the unnamed, unclaimed and disenfranchised are buried. There are no markers. It is an expanse of well-manicured grass with beautiful flowers, topiary and statuary where the city sends John and Jane Does and children who have passed in the foster care system. Cemetery documentation exists about the circumstances and possible identity of the individuals but families are hard pressed to find the specific spot where a person might be buried if they visit the field.

As part of a personal goal I adopted the role of sentry while in uniform. Tens of thousands of graves will never again be attended by living family members because genealogy lines have long disappeared or relatives unaware of where their ancestors are even located. I'm undecided as to whether there's an afterlife or whether the souls of the dead remain where their bodies reside but maybe my presence gave those who had been long forgotten some comfort.

As a home to generations of immigrants, it's any wonder we know where anyone is buried at all. Fortunately, Beacon Hill keeps meticulous records. The staff can usually find anyone who is known to be buried there. The service is necessary when matching the newly deceased with pre-paid plots but it's also important for those trying to find answers to questions about their origins. I used the service there long before taking the security job. Unlike the other cemetery where they wanted me to front the eternal care bill, Beacon Hill's records aren't on old, yellowed index cards. The system is automated. It's comforting to know that there is a place to visit my family even if they aren't quite "here" anymore.

Of course, other uses of the service involve tracking the famous and the infamous. Historic tours are frequent and informative but visitors sometimes come on their own quests for very personal reasons. I had occasion to play tour guide on days where not much was happening. It was always fun to drive people around to the place where someone in history was laid to rest and watch their reaction. It was both morbid and curious. I'd done the same thing many times with my wife when walking around New Orleans to see the graves of Marie Leveau (the Witch Queen of New Orleans) and pirate Jean Lafitte or the hundreds of Hollywood movie stars buried all over Los Angeles.

On other occasions it meant helping family find graves that they hadn't visited in a long time or had missed their funerals entirely. It was heart wrenching taking people to the site of their loved ones. Sometimes the family member was mistaken in where they thought the grave was. It took patience not to contradict them. I'd often help them look but would usually offer to take them to the office to have a proper records search done so that the location of the grave could be pinpointed precisely.

Many times we'd return to the spot where we'd been looking and find the grave either had no marker on it or was merely close by. The only appropriate thing was to offer them condolences, a box of tissues, and their privacy. For many it was the end of a long, hard, emotional journey. For me, I was in charge of driving the taxicab through hell and back. I never got used to it.

CHAPTER FIVE

VISITATION

The cemetery was most alive after the gates were opened in the morning. It was a beehive of activity while the dead slept, oblivious to those treading on the soil above. Fifteen hours of activity. Nearly all the staff was gone by 5PM. Some of the administrative staff remained – finishing up paperwork on plot deals, arranging for complete funeral services that would need to be implemented within the next two days and even cold calling. On the surface this sounds unsavory like lawyers who are ambulance chasers but I've come to appreciate such an approach because so many people never think about what they're going to do when they or a loved one dies unexpectedly. Without the sales staff shilling for business in advance it's unlikely there'd be much walk-up traffic. Hearses don't just arrive looking for a place to put a body. It takes serious planning.

It's traditionally been the domain of funeral homes. To survive, the cemeteries themselves have moved into the funeral planning business even partnering or buying faltering funeral homes to ensure uninterrupted planning and execution of ceremonies, burials and cremations. It's not a job I'd want, but it's damn necessary and I can only recommend shopping around and comparing prices if your circumstances allow it. If you leave it to the last minute, you will pay a hefty price and not just in the loss of a loved one.

A major part of that cost now involves the service. Many opt for a full ceremony at the cemetery using the Visitation Centre or mausoleum chapels as surrogates for a traditional church service. In a major city it can be cumbersome to have a funeral caravan going from funeral home, to church, to graveyard. Beacon Hill provides access to all three. Families can congregate once and stay for all aspects of the ceremony. One-stop-shop as it were.

The Visitation Centre staff was the last to leave every night. Rarely was there an evening where it wasn't open to one, two or even three services at once. That included two days of visitations, then the religious or ecumenical last rites and, finally, the interment on the grounds. These people were incredible because they were also responsible for getting death certificates, ordering caskets or urns, and embalming and dressing bodies not to mention catering, music (live or canned) and dealing with florists. A true steely constitution was necessary and a real love for the job. They were the last lines of interaction with hundreds of mourners every day and getting mourners to leave at the end of the night was often problematic.

No one wants to let a loved-one go. Visitations are the final goodbye. Once the lid is closed on the casket and the next day brings the funeral proper there is a defeated acceptance. Until then, families are determined to squeeze in more time with the dearly departed. Every mourner stretched out the allotted time until it was necessary to shake him or her loose so the staff could go home.

On rare occasions I was brought in as muscle. I never had to bounce anyone per se, but the staff used me as an excuse to clear the building. "Sorry, folks, security needs to clear the building and lock up for the night."

It usually got people motivated, well, at least the sober ones.

Inebriated people at a funeral are a bad combination of grief, anger, loss, and sadness. I'd never know which of these emotions was operating the human behind the booze at any given time. I saw a few people take swings at each other – usually over unresolved personal bullshit that had been brewing for years – but never at me. We'd ask that members of the party take care of this person and not allow them to drive.

COURAGE IN THE FACE OF DEATH

The residual effect of working at the cemetery is a mild form of PTSD. I am in no way saying it's similar to anything experienced by first responders, war vets or anyone whose life is both being threatened or having to witness threats perpetrated against others. I can imagine there's a tinge of it in the world of morticians, embalmers, funeral assistants and gravediggers. You cannot be around living beings and not be affected by their deaths no matter how far removed you try to be emotionally.

I spent my working hours "on" – that is, focused on tasks and patrolling my territory for escaped, urinating/shitting dogs and helping people with information. It was inconsequential in the grand scheme of things, unobtrusive and pedestrian in its execution. As long as there was something to do and I was occupied with one activity or another it was just an average day driving around in a car being Cemetery Cop.

But when I was alone and specifically alone at night my brain had its own ideas. Too much time to think, too much information to process. You could pretend the job was utilitarian but as the sun set the emotional balance would shift. Less authoritarian rule over the cemetery's occupants, and more metaphysical thoughts would crop up. The subconscious is insidious if left to its own devices.

It was in those moments of reflection I would face the prospect that death in all its manifestations was terribly, horrifically real. Philosophers and Zen masters can riff on for days about spirituality and the beauty of ascending or becoming one with the universe but not a single soul had ever returned and tapped me on the shoulder to say, "Hey, everything's cool on the other side."

We all believe differently. The most frequent question I'm asked is if there were ghosts at the cemetery. I'm no authority, but my interactions at the graveyard make me far more qualified than, say, some ghost hunting TV show where they run CCTV cameras for a sparse four nights in an old abandoned insane asylum and pick up one or two odd things. I spent the equivalent of five days a week at Beacon Hill for an entire year. I saw nothing unusual or out of the ordinary. I polled the other guards and staff some of whom had been there for a decade or more and unexplained occurrences was very few and very far between.

That's not to say I wasn't scared shitless and scarred psychically on several occasions. Despite knowing that I was always walking among the dead there was one or two occasions a week when I was taken by surprise. Jump scares in movies are nothing compared to wandering into a visitation room with all the lights off and coming face to face with a body sitting bolt upright in a coffin. I can imagine I looked like Don Knotts in *'The Ghost and Mr. Chicken'*. It was infrequent which is why when it did happen it was time to change the ol' underwear.

The problem was the same when entering the holding area and freezer where bodies were delivered and stored – sometimes five or six deep if it was a particularly bad week for mortality. When you're alone and there's gurneys filled with body bags the mind starts to go on defense.

The only mechanism I had to deal with any of this was convincing my brain that it was normal. It was the Circle of Life thing, yada, yada, yada. The heart, however, runs on an entirely different system of logic in that there is none. I am not ashamed to say that I lost my emotional composure three times while doing my job there.

The first time was not long after I'd started at the cemetery. Many times visitation for the deceased would wrap up around 9PM. As noted, the staff was very effective in getting the mourners and visitors out within about 30 minutes. They wanted to go home too. They'd been there all day preparing people for the coming interment and having to deal with all other matter of business in between visitations like arranging funerals for the remainder of the week or even a month away when families wanted to scatter cremated remains.

On one particular night the staff had a shortened visitation schedule for a family and everyone had cleared out by 8.30 PM. That allowed me to get in, secure the building (doors, windows, locks) and set the alarms. It was a 30-minute procedure because the building was massive and there were no less than three visitation rooms to go through. Sometimes all of them had caskets and flowers and memorial photos set up and ready for the next day's events which was the full funeral service.

On this night there was only one and it was in the biggest room – the church chapel which could hold a few hundred visitors. I always secured the chapel last as it was closest to the front doors and I would leave right after closing it up. I did my rounds checking the offices and the kitchen and the 'party' rooms where they served food and held wakes. There was also the massive basement that had a rather noisy elevator shaft and was very unsettling in the dark in its own right. Finally there were the exits to and from the garage where the fleet of hearses was parked before heading to the chapel.

I went through the side doors of the chapel, straight passed the coffin and to the perimeter doors where the hearses would park to take the deceased out to the cemetery. I secured the door's deadbolt and headed to a small room at the back where the audio/visual system was. Memorial films and slide shows are the newest addition to funeral services and many times the music was left playing from the visitation during the day. This night was no exception. The music was typically pastoral but it immediately caught me off guard as slightly different. These were lullabies and children's songs. I turned the music off and turned around to close the massive double doors to secure the room.

There, over top of this closed casket was an eight-foot by six-foot photograph of a smiling girl. She couldn't have been more than 3 or 4 years old. I looked around the room. The entire chapel was filled with balloons. There were hundreds of balloons floating on the ceiling waiting silently for tomorrow. While being engrossed in the tasks at hand I'd completely missed this. I walked back toward the coffin. The picture of this beautiful angel transfixed me. My heart sank. I didn't want this to be real.

I walked slowly up the centre aisle of the chapel and it was only then that I saw that on the back of every chair was a coloured sheet of paper with a typed note on each. I sat down in one of the chairs and looked at the first one. "You will never leave my heart, Lilly. I love you." It was signed by a 5 year-old from a nearby hospital. Tears began to well up. NO!!!

I moved over two seats. There was another message, another note from another kid from the same hospital. I was now in full crying mode. I moved from seat to seat, row on row. I read the message on the back of every chair. There were over 30 of them.

There are tissue boxes provided by the Visitation Centre staff in the chapel seats. I burned through a whole box. I stood up and walked to the casket. There were more pictures of this little angel on top. To one side there was a small table with literature on it; Brochures about childhood cancers and a donation envelope that is common practice where the family wishes to raise money in lieu of flowers as a memorial. Lilly had succumbed to brain cancer at 3 ½ years old. I sat back down in the front row and tried to take it all in. So young, so brave and the outpouring of love was unbelievable.

I was shaken out of my stupor by a call from dispatch doing their hourly check in on me. I explained that I was sidelined by one of the deceased. "10-4, buddy. We've all been there. Take your time."

There is no security guard handbook to deal with this type of scenario. Security training involves showing you how to handle someone having a heart attack or a bad fall. Post-mortem distress is classified under the 'suck it up, bitch' category. But you can never control how you might react to something. I've seen a lot of death that directly affected me. You never get used to it, but you do get an idea how to deal with it, and bounce back.

When it's someone else's tragedy that effects you there is no outlet. It's why it surprised me when it happened again. I now had a clear picture of what the loss of a small child would look it and what to expect. I did some psychological work on how to recognize the emotional triggers and how to defend myself.

But what about the death of a young teen? There was a 13 year-old boy that had taken his own life after being bullied mercilessly at school. That was a hard one for me as I'd been bullied all through public school and into my first year of high school. Even at my weakest, most depressed moments it never occurred to me to end my own life. My thoughts always leaned toward exacting revenge on the bullies. This boy didn't see it the same way.

I was told in advance that the funeral was going to be a shit show for traffic congestion. They were expecting over 1000 people. His entire school was expected to be there.

So I was removed from the ceremony itself and spent a few hours outside on foot directing people in and out of the Visitation Centre. Car and vanloads of adults with teenage kids on board, all kids who knew this young lad. Friends, schoolmates and most probably the bullies themselves. The injustice of the whole thing weighed on my mind the entire day.

About three-quarters of the way through the service I got a call from the Visitation staff related to a different matter entirely. They needed me to help them unload a rather heavy casket from a hearse for a service the following day. It required walking through the front doors and down a connecting hallway from the chapel where this teenager's ceremony was playing out.

I hadn't been near the building since earlier that morning. As I approached the front entrance there was a line-up. Hundreds of people were waiting to pay their respects. It was both heart warming and tragic that it had come to this. I squeezed through the doors where a crowd of people was congregated in the foyer talking to one of the funeral assistants. She was handing out superhero T-shirts.

Batman. Spider-Man. Superman.

Farther ahead the line-up was wending into the chapel. Everyone was dressed like a superhero. Some even wore the masks and capes. It was Felini-film surreal and unnerving. I ducked into a room to the left and shut the door behind me and started to cry. The feels were deep with this one. The costumes spoke volumes. This kid was looking for someone to save him, to be the shield, to stop the hurting.

This. Wasn't. Fair.

I was brought back to earth when a staff member came into the room, "You're not supposed to be in here."

I'd had run-ins with her before. She saw I'd been crying but didn't let up, "Get your shit together. Don't you have somewhere else to be?"

For the first and only time during my time at Beacon Hill I wished that it were her in that casket. I'm not sure how someone with so little empathy could do the job she did. None of the other staff I encountered were this way. Maybe it was mechanism for self-preservation. Some do strong and silent, others make inappropriate jokes about death and others just blank the pain and sorrow. I understand it but could never just turn the switch off. I have a limit to keeping a stiff upper lip. Sometimes these things happen and it teaches you about yourself and in this case, about other people.

The family survivors have the same battle. You can bottle it up and never deal with your feelings when a loved one dies, or you can let that river flow. The issue becomes control. When do you finally let go and deal with your grief? Some never do. It's evident by the number of people who practically live graveside and most times for people who've been dead decades. I've never been particularly attracted to the idea of sitting beside a tombstone and weeping for my dead relatives. Or praying. Or feeding them a metaphorical meal. All things considered equal, these are activities for the living. Penance? Flagellation? Atonement? Guilt? The dead have none of this to worry about. The survivors assign the significance of that grave or the urn housing someone's ashes to it. The moment the dead truly rest in peace is when their loved ones let go of that grief.

This was never more evident to me than an unbelievable incident that nearly caused me to turn in my badge and crawl under a blanket never to return to a cemetery ever again.

I was sitting in front of the Visitation Centre one morning having just checked with staff for the day's events. I was in my patrol car organizing some documents and getting ready to start my first patrol when I noticed an SUV pull up next to me on the right. A woman opened the driver's door and she had a beautifully decorated ceramic urn in hand – it was burgundy with gold inlay of dragons and some kind of inscription.

Unfortunately, she hadn't quite untangled herself from the SUV's seatbelt and as she began to step down from the vehicle the belt yanked her back and she lost her grip on the urn. Like some slow motion playback in a football game the urn went end-over-end and shattered on the pavement. I winced as I could hear, but could not see, the crash.

I opened my door and jumped out of the patrol car and ran around to the side where she was. There she was in a beautiful sequined tan dress on her hands and knees screaming as she ran her hands through the ashes and the ceramic glass strewn across the pavement. I kneeled beside her and put one hand on her shoulder. Tears were streaming down her face as she started sobbing uncontrollably still sifting the ashes through her fingers. I got up and ran to the front doors of the Visitation Centre and yelled in to the receptionist to get a broom and a dustpan as there was an urn broken in the parking lot.

I returned to the distraught woman who had put her hands up to her face to hide her disgrace and maybe disgust (it was hard to tell) over what had happened. She was chanting something and rocking back and forth. It sounded like a name. I tried to get her to look at me. I wasn't supposed to touch anyone on the job unless it was to administer First Aid but I forced her chin toward me and was horrified to see she had ash and blood all over her face…and in her eyes…and in her mouth. Without exaggeration, she looked like the white-faced demon from the movie The Grudge.

She began to stick her fingers down her throat to make herself vomit. She was regurgitating black goo onto her hand and down her arm. I nearly threw up. I held it together and moved a few steps away, grabbed my cellphone and dialed 911. Two funeral assistants came out right behind me. One grabbed the woman and forced her to her feet and took her inside the V/C while the other began the unenviable task of sweeping up the remains. I looked down and I was covered in ash. My black pants were now smoky grey. My white shirt was now streaked with black. There was blood on the cuff of one arm.

I looked at the funeral assistant and said, "Is this stuff toxic?"

She shook her head, "Not really unless you've got a habit of snorting it like Keith Richards. Any bacteria are burned off during cremation. This is literally charcoal now."

"I feel awful for this woman."

"We get one or two of these a year. We have an interment option for families where we will pick up cremated remains and bring them here for scatterings or memorial services. People either want to save a buck or they don't trust that we'll handle the ashes properly and then something like this happens. We warn against it but sometimes you can't change their minds."

"How do you clean this stuff off? I don't want to do a 15 hour shift looking like I just walked out of a coal mine."

The assistant said she had something for that and went inside with the remains of the woman's relative in a cardboard box. I had to wait for the ambulance. The FA returned with a spray bottle and a fine brush – the kind that umpires use to sweep the dirt off home base in a baseball game. She shook me down and then with the spray bottle and a fabric softener dryer sheet managed to get almost all the ash off me. My shirt was the worse for wear, as it was now an off-white colour. I was creeped out knowing that I was wearing remnants of a dead person.

The ambulance finally arrived and I explained to the EMS paramedics what had happened. They both looked at each other. Apparently, this was a new one on them. They went inside the Visitation Center and it took them about 30 minutes to clean the woman up and treat her for the cuts and give her liquids to neutralize the ash she had ingested.

You can't walk away from something like that and not be affected. This is the first I've spoken of it. My wife always knew when something bad happened at work, but I never talked about this one. It gave me nightmares and, as I said, made me question my future as a Cemetery Cop.

CHAPTER SIX

THESE ARE THE WORKING HOURS

With my training complete I was handed a two-week schedule that was a rotation of myself and two other guards on alternating days – sometimes four on and three off or two on, one off, two on, etc. With the exception of a two-day traffic duty job north of the city where a bridge was being replaced I never worked any other jobs during the entire year as a security guard. I was embedded at the cemetery and remained there. Other guards were moved in and out of condos, shopping malls, etc. but I was wanted there full-time as Billy felt the staff at Beacon Hill deserved reliable, friendly security faces they could call on and not have to baby-sit them on a daily basis. Once I figured out the rhythm of my routine the entire cemetery staff knew where and when I'd be available for any need.

I have a strong work ethic. People pay me to be effective and reliable and in return I am. It's how you keep a roof over your head and you never take that for granted. I missed a half-day's work in that entire year and it was because I misread my schedule. I received a rather abrupt phone call from the dispatcher when I didn't show up to get my patrol car one morning. It was the exception. Otherwise I was never late, and always prepared. I carried a knapsack wherever I went and added things to that kit as incidents and encounters demanded. Initially I carried my lunch, some music to listen to, work gloves (held over from my days working on the rail yard), a flashlight, a notebook and my security report book, cemetery maps and eventually had to add Kleenex, a First Aid kit, a cigarette lighter, WD-40, and lock de-icer. We'll get to those later.

The uniform was typical of all security guards: white shirt, black pants, tie, applets, black loafers, a pen and any combination of walkie-talkie (to reach dispatch) and smart phone (to communicate with the cemetery managers and supervisors). I also brought along a Samsung tablet – a gift from my mother one Christmas. It allowed me to get on the internet during lunch/dinner breaks to stave off the monotony. Usually I just did crossword puzzles because they weren't nearly as distracting or engrossing. They helped pass the time when things were slow at the cemetery. But a slow day was rare unless it was raining or snowing, but even then there was always a burial. Always.

FIRST DAY ON THE JOB

My first official day at Beacon Hill patrolling without Billy was a Sunday. Technically the cemetery was closed Sundays in that there was no office staff and only grounds staff if there was a burial. Those were generally held off until the Monday following if at all possible. That left one maintenance guy on site for emergencies that I came to know as Lopez. His job was to clean up the 40-gallon garbage cans that hadn't been emptied since the Friday before. He also did repair work on the equipment that might need repair, building repairs and cleaning bathrooms in some instances and occasionally set up grave digging equipment so it was ready first thing Monday morning when there was a full compliment of maintenance guys on hand. He was an amazing help and confidante when I had issues on the grounds. The first day on site was no exception.

It was starting to turn from summer to fall with many days of rain so the ground was beginning to get soggy and muddy but the sun was bright and warm. I was driving around watching everything like an eager hawk, as I was nervous and not sure what to expect with only the supposed tall tales Billy had filled my head with during orientation.

On this day as I pulled around the cul-de-sac in the cemetery valley a woman jogger and her teenage son came running up the pathway from the ravine. She was out of breath and waved frantically at me. Both of them came up to the window. "There's something in the ravine you need to see," said the woman. Her son stood behind her nodding his head.

I put the car in park, rolled up the windows, stepped out and locked it up. She led the way and I followed. Beyond the gate that I'd opened earlier that day was the trail down into the ravine but there were two paths you could take before crossing the river. She took the left one and followed the water for quite a while before coming to a foot bridge that led across the water and into a bigger valley.

"Look!"

She was pointing at several pieces of paper lying on the bridge, splayed out in the warm sun. There was no wind that day or the documents would have been blown into the water. I approached cautiously and kneeled down to take a closer look. There was a sale brochure for an upcoming condominium project with pages half torn out as well as one from a bank plus some three-ring lined paper with a stream of hand written words on both sides. I pushed them around on the wooden bridge with the butt-end of my walkie-talkie. In plain English on the lined paper you could clearly see a checklist of things to do:

1) Call Mr. XXXX at Bank Y
2) Call Mr. ZZZZ at Bank R
3) Call Mrs. JJJJ at Bank F
4) Phone Daily Herald newspaper
5) Issue threat about the death of Mr. XXXX. Phone number 555-444-3333
6) Passport
7) Plane tickets (3)
8) Solidarity, brotherhood
9) Death to the U.N.
10) Mayors dead in London, Toronto, Ottawa, New York, Jamaica

I stood up and tried not to panic. The woman and the teenage boy were already doing that for me. I took their information, which they gave freely, so I was pretty sure they didn't plant the pages there. The woman said she'd actually seen them off to one side of the bridge but put them in plain sight in case she couldn't find anyone from the cemetery to take a look. She thanked me for taking care of the issue. I assured her that this was probably a hoax and that I'd get the proper authorities to take a look just in case.

I escorted them back to my patrol car and advised them that there might be a call from the police in the future. They thanked me again and jogged off. Fearing that someone else would stumble across the scene or move the items, I grabbed my work gloves and the plastic bag that my lunch was wrapped in and headed back to the bridge. After taking photos of the scene with my cellphone I put the pages and a ball point pen I'd found at the front of the footbridge into the plastic bag and headed immediately to the maintenance yard where Lopez was washing some mud covered ATV Gators.

"Lopez, we've got a problem," I said in a serious tone.

"Hey, man, it's all cool. It's your first day. I'm here to help."

I poured the contents of the plastic bag onto the trunk of my patrol car and pointed at the one with death threat list on it. Lopez was from Honduras and his complexion was fairly sun-baked. As his eyes darted across the page his face became ashen.

"Holy shit. This is serious. We have to call the police!"

"I know. I can't believe this is happening during my first day on my first shift. Ever. I'm gonna get fired for this for sure," I was starting to panic.

"No. No. No. I'll vouch for you. You better call dispatch and get them to decide what needs to be done."

I got my walkie-talkie out and buzzed the dispatcher.

"Yeah, what's up. It's not your time to check in yet. Don't tell me. A dog pissed on a flower bed and you don't know what to do?"

I wasn't impressed with the attitude but I guess they'd heard everything from newbies over years and years of shifts. "I just found what looks like a bomb threat at Beacon Hill."

There was no sound at the other end.

"Hello? Did you hear me? There were documents left in the ravine that look like a rough outline for a terrorist attack."

"Christ, man. Do not say that. This is an open channel. Here's what you're going to do. You're going to call the police, then you're going to go back and secure the area. There's police tape in the tool kit in the trunk of the patrol car. Cordon off the area and wait for them to arrive. After they've been there, buzz me back and give me an update. Do not leave the site."

"Got it."

Lopez had heard the entire conversation. He was now on his cell phone to the cemetery manager. Simultaneously, I had dialed 9-1-1. I gave them my badge number, my company affiliation and explained in short bursts what had been found and by whom.

There wasn't time to post police tape at the scene as three patrol cars came through the closest gate about two minutes later, sirens blaring. I met the first car and the officer introduced himself. I explained that I'd made the call and showed them what I'd found. Everyone stepped out of their cars and crowded around as I placed the documents on the hood of the first patrol car.

Two officers ran over every page wearing rubber gloves. A call was made to their dispatch and a conversation was hatched between him and his supervisor. Meanwhile, one of the other officers began taking info from me and copying down information about the jogger and her son as they were going to have to speak to them both.

The lead officer asked, "Can you show us where the documents were found?"

"Absolutely. Please follow me." I headed off in my patrol car and one car followed me. The other two remained near the gate talking to Lopez.

Two officers and myself headed down the ravine toward the river. They weren't happy about it. It was muddy and wet. We got to the bridge and they walked around it and over it to the other side looking at the access point, the surrounding bush and brush. It didn't appear like there was anything else there. They took notes. One took some cellphone pictures. The first officer wanted me to email him the shots I had taken before I'd moved the paper. I took down his vitals and fired them off right there.

We returned to our vehicles and the officer advised me that it was an incomplete piece to a bigger puzzle. They now had a task force working on these types of things full time. It was becoming routine, in fact, now that everyone was on high alert for terrorists. It didn't make me feel any better. Who the hell put these documents here? And what if they come back?

"Call us again if there's anything else suspicious. Anything," said the lead officer. "Give them my badge number and tell them you were instructed to call. They'll track me down. For now, we're going to hand everything over to the task force unit. You may get a call." With that he placed the stash of documents into a plastic folder and into a briefcase locked in the trunk of his vehicle.

They left with the other two cruisers in tow a few minutes later. I called my dispatcher and gave him the run down. "Write everything down in an incident report. Email those photos to the owner of the security company and your detail supervisor. They might want to debrief you at a later date."

No one ever did. Not even the police. It became a non-incident in the general scheme of things. So either the police thwarted some careless terrorists or the whole thing was a hoax perpetrated by kids or a drunken passer-by. Who knows? I came to not question these things after awhile as most of these incidents were deemed "business as usual" by staff and my security company.

VOODOO THINGS

As mentioned, the beginning of the day was the most hectic and nerve racking because it involved opening the entire cemetery before 7AM as per management's request. The priority was the perimeter gates followed by the buildings – both employee related and public access. When the weather was good and everything went according to plan I could open the gates before the allotted time. But when things went wrong, they could go really wrong.

There was a pedestrian walkway at the farthest end of Section 3. It was a bit of a hike from the road and Billy had shown me how to cut some time by using the walkway itself as its own access road. It allowed me to drive right up to the two gates – one was a double wrought iron gate, the other was a gated door for bicycle and wheelchair access directly beside it.

The trick to getting the patrol car onto this walkway was making sure you didn't drive on any of the grass or burial markers that ran along the left and right sides. The car was exactly the width of the walkway. If you moved the steering wheel at all in either direction you'd leave tire tracks down the centre of all the gravestones and/or the grass in between each. My trainer, Billy, had a habit of leaving tracks every shift.

Management was quick in catching on to this play and introduced two very large standing stones at the entrance to the walkway – making it nearly impossible to navigate the car between them. I said nearly impossible. No one counted on my ability to navigate a vehicle in very confined spaces. My two years of professional driving at the rail yard taught me how to negotiate postage stamp manoeuvres. If I came at the entrance perfectly straight I could squeeze the patrol car between the rocks with an inch to spare on each side.

The issue, of course, was reversing the car back out. That involved a steady hand and reliance on mirrors and an open driver's door to watch where the placement of at least one standing rock was to get my bearings. On only one occasion did I ever touch one of the standing stones. No harm done. Billy, who had been guarding the cemetery for years, didn't fair as well. He took the running board out of the bottom of at least three vehicles. You could never do it in a hurry. He was always in a hurry.

This particular gated entrance was a favourite of joggers as you could start there and spend a good hour or so making your way to the farthest gate and back again for a pretty good workout. If I was fast enough I could open every gate in the cemetery and make it to the farthest side as they ran by on their return trip. Woe to the guard who didn't get these two gates opened before 7AM. It happened on occasion especially on snowy or icy mornings where the locks on the gates were frozen from the previous night's weather.

After many of these mornings I learned to carry with me lock de-icer, WD40 (which works to melt ice as well) and a cigarette lighter. The trick was to warm the lock up enough to get the key inside and then spray the whole mechanism with WD40 to get the tumblers to turn over. Every guard had a different method. One guard, I was told, used to just back the patrol car up to the gate and let the muffler exhaust heat the locks. That sounded like a disaster waiting to happen. When I was faced with this situation I would remove all the locks from every gate and keep them in the car the entire day so that they were warm when I locked up at night.

On one particular morning I got to the Section 3 entrance to find a garbage bag on the inside of the gates. What kind of asshole would dump their garbage into a cemetery especially with a public bus stop and waste bin only 10 feet from the entrance? I went to move the bag and noticed it was sitting on a pile of coins. Loonies and Twonies and quarters strewn all over the walkway. Nice. Coffee money.

I couldn't open the pedestrian gates until I moved the bag. So I did. It clanked. I shook it up and down. It sounded like glass but not exactly. It was more like a heavy, deeper ceramic sound. I was intrigued. Curiosity got the better of me and I carefully tore the bag open with both hands near the top. As I created a gaping hole in the plastic I saw feathers. I made the hole even bigger and jumped back, dropping the bag. The feathers were attached to the body of a chicken. Its head was gone. What the hell? Now I was going to have to report this.

I got on the walkie-talkie to dispatch and told them what I'd found. The dispatcher didn't seem surprised in the least, "Let me know if you find any goats' heads. They usually leave one or two on top of graves every year around this time. Don't get any blood on you. Hahaha."

Double what the hell! Apparently, it was normal to have practitioners of Haitian Vodou, Santeria Lucumi,

Hoodoo or even West African Vodun perform their syncretic or amalgamated religious ceremonies in the cemetery. Unfortunately, that also includes animal sacrifice. I expected this type of thing in New Orleans but never in an urban Canadian city.

There was an automated outhouse beside the gates. It was fully functioning with electricity and heat/air conditioning for the cemetery's maintenance crew to stop them from taking unnecessary and lengthy breaks driving back and forth to the maintenance yards just to take a piss. I stepped inside and washed my hands. I returned to my patrol car and dug out a pair of gloves from my knapsack. I put them on and disposed of the garbage bag in the waste bin beside the outhouse. I called the cemetery ground supervisor and let him know what I'd found. They would send a crew over immediately to dispose of the bag. Last thing they wanted was the public to find it. With this era of social media the dead chicken would end up on Instagram or Facebook in no time.

THE CONCRETE SCENE

The worst morning I ever had at Beacon Hill was the day I arrived to open the main gates on Beacon Hill Road. Behind me, waiting patiently, was a cement truck that needed to deliver wet cement to the cenotaph renovation going on in the military officers' section. The cemetery was adding a new walkway and common area for people to sit and view the graves of fallen and deceased soldiers.

I swung the massive gates inward and returned to the patrol car. I drove through the open gateway and pulled off to one side, waving the driver through so he could get to the work site before the mad rush from maintenance workers, office staff and others began.

He signaled his thanks and turned the truck toward the entrance. But he had been parked closely against the curb leading into the entrance so the front end, and then the rear wheels all jumped the curb as he moved into the driveway proper. The angle of his turning radius was too short and he hit a 12 foot stone pillar with the two sets of back tires on the inside of the turn. I watched in horror as the truck took out a three foot section of the pillar and the four hundred pound wrought iron gate attached to it.

The noise was horrendous as the massive 15 foot gate bent and buckled like a pretzel. He'd managed to destroy a beautiful Gothic 100 year-old cemetery entrance. The back tires on the truck went flat and a portion of the truck's fender was bent back like the lid of a tin can. It was like someone had taken a can opener and peeled the side of the truck. The driver stopped the vehicle a dozen feet past me with the belching sound of air brakes.

He got out and cursed in a foreign language. It might have been Italian or maybe it was Portuguese. Either way I could tell he was not pleased. Neither was I. This was on my watch and now I had to call everyone in charge to report this: dispatch, management, maintenance staff, you name it. And now my morning ritual was completely fucked. The gates were not going to be opened on time. I expected a flurry of complaints to Beacon Hill's head office from the precious joggers whose steps-per-minute were going to be blown out. All I could think of was "bite me."

Two other trucks followed after the cement truck from the same construction company. Their lead Captain came and spoke to me. I told him what happened. They were worried I was going to call the police. I told them I didn't need to do that as they were here on behalf of the cemetery as per their contract. They'd have to deal with the wrath of the site manager instead. I waved them on. The cement truck limped over to the cenotaph site and they got to complete their work.

The delay set me back about 45 minutes. Fortunately, other staff who had arrived not long after saw the disaster and made sure all the gates were opened on my behalf. The tide of whiney joggers was reduced to a few entitled doctors and lawyers who were inconvenienced with their First World problems. Boo hoo.

The maintenance staff came out to look at the gate. The stone pillar was an easy fix but the wrought gate – the biggest one in the cemetery – was another matter altogether. These gates weren't cheap and they weren't easy to make. A new one would have to be created and it had to match its counterpart attached to the opposite pillar so that they were still a matching set. Worse still is that the Beacon Hill monogram was hand crafted into the ironwork. The entranceway was now wide open. Maintenance was going to have to jerry-rig something for me to close at the end of the night.

But there was still the matter of the cement truck. It wasn't driving out of there on its own steam, not with four flat tires. So when the construction crew finally emptied the truck of cement they called in a towing company to come get the beast. Alas, when the heavy-duty tractor trailer-sized tow truck arrived it was too large to fit through the entrance. It was the kind they used to tow other 18-wheelers. They needed to send the next size down. It took two hours to find another one that could battle the traffic through the city to where we were.

It took another hour to rig up a system to get the cement truck off the ground so that it could roll on its remaining wheels. I needed to call in the ground supervisor, Mark, to help me with traffic control. To get both trucks out of the cemetery they were going to have to drive straight across Beacon Hill Road partially through the entrance gates on the opposite side of the road, turn and reverse and then ease into oncoming traffic to clear the entranceway – and the surviving gate.

Fortunately, the tow truck driver was a little smarter than the cement truck driver had been. He made it look simple. But the repair job on the entrance was going to take weeks.

CHAPTER SEVEN

UNIVERSAL SOLDIERS

The work honeymoon lasted a few weeks as I attempted to recall my security training from two years before and the wisdom Billy imparted on me in two short days driving around the cemetery. Navigating the roads was the biggest challenge. It was easy to see how people could get lost in there especially as night fell.

Landmarks were important in finding your way around. I pretty much knew where all the gates were as they generally dotted the outside perimeter of the entire cemetery. Finding monuments, crypts, tombs and buildings wasn't as easy. I carried a map in my breast pocket so that if staff called I could zero in on where they needed me to be immediately. Other times it was decided in advance.

Due to the size and age of Beacon Hill it was a destination for the burial of many of Canada's VIPs. I got my first exposure to such a funeral less than a week after the shooting of soldier Nathan Cirillo on Parliament Hill in Ottawa.

One of Canada's most celebrated Brigadier-Generals was being laid to rest and it was going to be a large military deal. Soldiers at arms, 21-gun salute, and all the honours afforded a man who'd seen combat and run missions during World War II, the Suez Crisis and the Korean War. There would be representatives from a dozen different Canadian Forces bases and reps from Ottawa to commemorate his life.

With the size of the procession and its participants, there was a nervous tension associated with the proceedings so soon on the heels of the attack in Ottawa. The cemetery was going to be crawling with military personnel – most of whom would be unarmed. The local police and the RCMP were brought in on two consecutive days to sweep the cemetery for all manner of hiding places and objects that could conceal incendiary devices.

To that end the standard 40 gallon oil drum garbage cans were completely removed from the section of the cemetery where the Brigadier General would be interred. Maintenance staff were all interviewed and vetted and then re-assigned to a different section of the cemetery. Some of the other funerals for that day were even rescheduled to not coincide with this one.

The head of my security company, the assignment manager and even the mobile supervisor were brought in and debriefed along with myself to explain how the commitment ceremony was going roll out. In a rare move we would had three of our guards on site – one watching the gate with the procession, the other at the opposite gates in that section. Then there was myself shadowing the lead vehicle containing the Brigadier- General from a road that would run parallel to the one they were on. I got the shadowing position because it was my shift that day. I guess it never occurred to anyone that the guy with the least experience should have been on the quiet gate monitoring traffic. But, no, they threw me into the thick of it.

They weren't concerned. The local police service was sending in two teams of officers to patrol the grounds and act as defense at the graveside itself – one group was on bicycles, the other in patrol cars for a total of 10 officers. The site of the plot for the interment was against a War Memorial retaining wall with an alley behind it for pedestrian and vehicular access to some adjacent condominiums. Officers from the Emergency Task Force were ensconced on the condominium side of the wall. Another team of officers who looked like Navy Seals or Black Ops were not far down from them. One team set up a sniper look out on top of the retaining wall. They were in direct contact with a helicopter that sat above the cemetery for the entire funeral service, the voices from their walkie-talkie chatter echoing down the condo alleyway.

I was scared shitless. The cemetery staff was unruffled. It was all in a day's work.

What no one was prepared for was the weather. It was overcast with sunny breakthroughs every few minutes and the wind had kicked up as well. The rain came and went in cycles. The ground stayed damp the entire time.

I was instructed to wait with the security guard near the gate where the procession would enter – car ready to ride shadow along an access road that paralleled the property fence. At a certain juncture the funeral vehicles would head up a hill on a more accessible road and I'd be able to mimic their drive as I would only separated by 50 feet of grass. I could match their speed, which was very slow. The two roads would eventually meet. I was to let them go ahead of me and I was to stop and block both roads at the junction once the final vehicle had passed – ensuring that no one from the public could access the area where the grave was. The security guard at the farthest gate would drive in from the opposite side and block that road from access as well. We had practiced the manoeuvre several times that morning.

I was standing and making small talk with the security guard at the procession gate as we waited for the event to start. We started re-directing pedestrians and cyclists in preparation. Then we saw the vehicles coming down the ridiculously angled slope on Beacon Hill Road; A police motorcycle escort that blocked the road in both directions as the cars turned into the cemetery was leading them. I got in my car and moved down the property gate road to be in position. I'd be able to watch the cars turn up the access road in my rear view mirror. We all had our walkie-talkies standing by to receive any further directives.

The road I was on had a curve in it. I wouldn't be able to see the procession until they were almost at the cut off for the access road. It was taking a while. To my left I watched more cars rolling down Beacon Hill to swarm the gate behind me. There were 32 vehicles in all. I hadn't seen the first limousines pull in because I was moving into place. Then I looked in my rear view mirror. Directly behind me was a massive green armoured personnel vehicle. Six huge wheels and two soldiers popping out of the top scoping out the surroundings like a whack-a-mole game. It was the kind of truck you see the UN drive into war zones. This was the lead vehicle and they didn't turn onto the access road as planned, they were coming right at me.

The side roads in Beacon Hill are only wide enough for one vehicle. I was now in the way. I pulled onto the grass and watched them pass. Being towed behind it was a cannon. I later found out it was a semi-restored 105mm

Howitzer from the Second World War. It was slightly larger than the two we had on site near the other military graves. The Brigadier-General's coffin was fixed to the top of the gun barrel and covered with a Canadian flag. I stopped my car, got out and saluted. It seemed the appropriate thing to do.

Then it hit me. The procession had gone up the access road without them. I was the only security between them and the grave site. I called the other guards and told them what was going on. The supervisor instructed me to follow at a respectable distance behind the APC and the Brigadier-General and to resume the original plan once they passed the road merge. I did as I was told. The military vehicle went on ahead and met up with the remainder of the procession in front of the grave. I pulled the car into the middle of the road and parked it across the intersection. I was to stay with the car and re-direct pedestrians and cyclists like we'd done at the gate. The public was to have no access to the proceedings. Two of the police cyclists arrived to help. We got chatting a bit. Unlike the funeral staff, this was not business as usual for them. They were generally dealing with J-walkers, people parking illegally and a mess of other traffic infractions. They were both happy to be doing something that broke up their monotony for a change.

The rain returned. The families and other people in the procession were smart enough to sport umbrellas. One of the local military academies had shown up by bus. There were easily 40 of them. Young men and women dressed to the 9's. Cadets in training and clearly excited to be part of something, anything that allowed them to participate. There were several with white rifles. Reveille was played in the Brigadier-General's honour. A speech was given which was inaudible from where I stood. "Amazing Grace" on bagpipes came next. Then it was the 21-gun salute. The curiosity seekers that hung out next to the bicycle cops and myself recoiled from the noise. In short order the whole thing was over.

The cadets scattered. Some returned to the bus, others headed past me to seek a public transit alternative. Other military types returned to their vehicles. Both a Sergeant and a Major came toward me and shook my hand thanking me for my help and the help from the security company. They did the same with the police. It was quite an honour to have been involved in such a ceremony and more importantly trusted with such an important role.

Remembrance Day followed not long after this. It was a wholly different affair held at the Gothic mausoleum where a WWI air force hero was honoured in a new tradition sponsored by the Canadian Air Force. The cemetery had been called upon to host the event for Canadian military flying aces while other cemeteries and city ceremonies focused on foot soldiers and militia.

Beacon Hill's management was happy to oblige as it gave the cemetery a very public profile in the media and was a break from the usual grief-stricken events normally held on site. Speeches were given and there was another 21-gun salute performed by members of Canadian Forces Base Borden cadets. It was a brilliantly sunny day so there were a lot of visitors on hand.

Shortly after the 11AM two minutes of silence a squadron of World War II airplanes flew over in formation tipping their wings toward us as they passed. The entire ceremony took about an hour and the atmosphere was hopeful and filled onlookers with plenty of national pride.

MAN DOWN

Unlike the military funeral which celebrated the high water marks of a very long and fulfilled life, there were also the truly tragic funerals of people cut short in the prime of their lives. That type of ceremony has a different energy about it. All funerals are sad occasions but some are blanketed with a foreboding pall. It's as if the deceased themselves hold onto whatever was haunting them in life.

One such ceremony involved a fire fighter that was brought in by procession from north of the city. I was again called on to escort the deceased who had been carried in on the top of a fire engine and draped in a Canadian flag. Service workers that die on the job are very upsetting and humbling. People giving their lives to save others. It's a calling and a courage I do not possess.

But more tragically is when a first responder dies not in the line of duty but due to suicide. This fire fighter was young at only 32 years old. He had been 8 years on the force. The mourners were devastated and rightly so. No one was talking about his long and dedicated service to his vocation. They talked about the sudden, unexpected loss and the devastation his death was leaving on those he left behind. Suicide was never mentioned. I was told about it in the preparation meeting for the event.

His fellow firemen were pallbearers. This was the Honour Guard. They were dressed in ceremonial uniform including white gloves, carrying his casket across the wet grass and staining their pants with mud and water. They didn't care about that. There was a man down who tragically rang the last bell prematurely.

The Fire Chief handed something to the man's next of kin. Maybe she was his wife. I don't know. I was later told it was his badge and name tag. Another fireman – one of the pallbearers - read something out loud. I couldn't hear what he was saying. I expect it was something inspirational and paid respect to a friend who'd lost his way. Rain was pouring down and I was upwind beside my patrol car keeping an eye on the curious onlookers who wanted to know what was going on.

"Did he die in the line of duty?"

"No. It was an illness."

"Oh."

I can't even imagine what they were all going through. It's one thing to consciously challenge death every day on the job, it's another to invite it in. To people like this man who are in distress I hope they can seek help and find support in their co-workers and family to find strength to battle poor health or mental illness or substance issues. I didn't know this man's situation but there should have been a better ending to his story.

The ceremonial bell rang in three sequences of three and a bagpiper played his best out-of-tune rendition of "Amazing Grace" as the rain had thrown the instrument completely out of tune. The mourners slowly scattered back to their cars and trucks. There was a wake planned at the Visitation Centre and most headed in that direction.

That evening I noticed there were still firemen milling about in the parking lot of the Visitation Centre. The rain had stopped and the clouds parted for a last burst of sunshine. There was a large white cube van where there hadn't been before. As I rolled down the incline in my patrol car from the back end of Section 1 down to the V/C parking lot I realized everyone on foot was holding a freshly cracked bottle of Molson Canadian beer. Upon further inspection there was a guy in shorts and a T-shirt pulling beer out of a box from the back of the van. I rolled past the entourage and smiled and waved.

Without second thought I got on the phone to the site manager and filled him in.

"There are approximately 20 firemen drinking in the V/C parking lot."

"Everyone?"

"They've all got beer in their hand. I must assume their consuming them," I reported.

"Keep an eye on them for now. We don't want anyone drinking and driving. If it looks like they're getting out of hand, call 911."

"10/4. Vernon out."

I continued my rounds and returned to the spot about an hour later and noticed that the white van had left. However, on the same approach road there were seven fire fighters still milling about an overturned garbage can. One individual was standing in the centre of the road with his pants down around his ankles. I pulled up next to two, clearly, intoxicated fire fighters who were still holding beer bottles.

Me: Sir, I see you are having a really good time here. Do you have a designated driver?

Fireman #1: Oh, we can all drive! Firetrucks! Toot! Toot!

Me: I'm sure you can, but....wait, that guy's arm is bleeding.

Fireman #2: Don't worry about him. He's a fucking idiot. He's the one that drives the fire truck!

Me: No one's driving a fire truck tonight, I'm afraid. Do I need to call someone to come and get all of you?

Fireman #1: No, no. We're good. [proceeds to put his jacket on upside down and inside out]

Me: I'll call you guys a cab.

Fireman #2: He can fire the drive truck!!

I drove past them and around the corner so they couldn't see me. I got on the horn to dispatch this time.

"I've got a situation here with seven very drunk fire fighters near the V/C parking lot."

"You're absolutely sure they're drunk?" the dispatcher asked.

"Yes, I saw them drinking an hour ago from a cargo van loaded with beer. The site manager had me stand down but now one of them is disrobing, and he's bleeding from his left arm."

"Call the site manager again and get permission to drop the hammer. We can't let them get into a vehicle. Don't let them know what you're doing or they could get belligerent."

"10-4. Beacon Hill out."

I turned the car around and headed back to the location so I could watch them while I called 911 and report their activity except they were gone. I patrolled the walkways and road access in and around the V/C. I expanded my search to other areas. I spent 20 minutes seeing if they were still on site. They had left the premises somehow under my nose. All that remained was one of their cars in the parking lot - thankfully - and an empty two-four of beer outside the front doors of the V/C.

I entered the V/C and had the cleaning staff go out and get the beer bottles. I warned them to not allow any firefighters back in the building – not even to pee - and if they saw anyone to call me immediately. Thankfully no call came. I assume the seven distraught and inebriated friends had gone back to their city of origin to resume their dangerous lives without their fallen friend.

CHAPTER EIGHT

OTHER DUTIES AS ASSIGNED

My security job wasn't always relegated to being in a patrol car in the field. It also included doing work directly for the cemetery support staff. This came about during times when the full staff compliment was reduced because the cemetery was extremely busy with events or on weekends when staffing was minimal.

I enjoyed the change of pace and the staff were far easier to deal with than the emotionally over reactive public with the exception of the one time I had to sit with a receptionist for a week straight after her ex broke the conditions of his restraining order. Management was afraid he was going to show up on site and do her harm. He never materialized but I had a head shot of the guy pasted to the dashboard of the patrol car for nearly a month after that.

HELLOWE'EN

I lost the scheduling lottery for doing security on Halloween. It's possibly the most angst-ridden night at cemeteries all over the world. It's a battle between religious belief, superstition, and drunk people in costumes wanting to prove something – whether it be how long they can stay in the creepy graveyard or just to be assholes by smashing glass and tipping headstones over. That makes it an insurance liability not just for damage but personal injury. You simply cannot have people wandering around inside the cemetery after the gates close in the dark.

But management took no chances on this night of shenanigans. The shift becomes dangerously long as we didn't just lock the gates at the end of the night as usual – we had to baby sit the empty property well into the witching hour. Fortunately, I would have re-enforcements.

With the cemetery being split into three massive zones there would be a guard for each section. The two relief guards were to show up at sundown. In the fall that meant 5:30 PM or so – the week before the clocks would go back an hour.

One guard came in his own vehicle. He was a retired senior named Larry doing security part-time for some extra pocket money. The second guard was named Akande who arrived at 6PM on foot from a nearby job guarding a construction site. The plan was to clear and lock each section with one of us inside. I had the master keys and would drive back and forth through each section every hour to check up on Larry and Akande.

The temperature had plummeted by closing time and it had started to rain. I sent Larry out to the back 40 where he could patrol the section of the cemetery with the least amount of foot traffic. It was all hills and it was on the opposite side of the ravine so people weren't going to be too anxious to make work for themselves terrorizing the cemetery in the dark or walking up steep hills in the rain.

With Akande on foot I left him closest to all the mausoleums. The security company wanted him patrolling on foot. That was cruel and unusual especially in light of it being his second shift that day. No one could patrol that much area on foot and manage to be effective. I told him to stick by the mausoleums closest to the entrance gates – it was the only place people could break into that section of the cemetery if at all.

The other reason was that he was scared. No, not scared, terrified. He was a nervous wreck. He didn't want to be left alone. He was visibly shaking from the thought of being in among the dead after dark. He was Nigerian and had some seriously ingrained beliefs about death. This was a handicap to us being effective as a security unit.

I called dispatch, "For Chrissake, they've sent me a guy who is afraid of his shadow. He's practically in tears here because he thinks zombies or something are going to come get him. Is there no one else I can get tonight?"

"Negative. He was the only extra body available to help you. Most of the guards are pulling tag team shifts at shopping malls and school properties."

Fuck.

I hoped and prayed it would be a quiet night. I sent Akande into one of the mausoleums to stay warm. He had an iPhone so I told him to listen to music or something to keep occupied. He was useless to me. Larry and I would have to patrol the grounds on our own. I couldn't be worried about this guy doing his job. He needed to step down. He'd get paid regardless.

"You want me to stay in here?" Akande pointed to the mausoleum foyer.

"Yes. You'll be warm. It's well lit and quiet."

"What is in this building?"

Oh, here we go, I thought to myself. "Bodies. There are dead bodies in there, Akande."

"Oh, no, no, no, sir. I cannot be in there," he said as he backed away from the door.

"Well you can't stand out here, Akande. It's too cold and you're afraid. What will you do if something really does happen?"

"I might die of fright," he shot back.

"You won't die from anyone buried here but you could die if you're too scared to defend yourself against a drunk person or someone that's violent."

"I am a good security guard. I work outside every day. 18 years a security guard. I do good work."

"I'm not saying you don't," I reassured him. "But you're now unfocused. You are worried about dead people. They cannot hurt you."

"You do not know this," he said narrowing his eyes and staring directly into mine. He almost had me going.

"Are you a religious man, Akande?"

"Yes, I was raised to believe that the dead are sacred and that we must respect their spirit."

"Fair enough. But I do not believe and for me to understand how we can make it through until the end of the night with you doing your job effectively, I need to understand why you are scared."

"No one has ever asked me this," he said as he contemplated my words. "I come from a very small village in Nigeria. In it we know everyone from the day we are born until we die. This village of people is family. We love and care for them all their lives. When they pass on we celebrate their lives as good, humble people. But here, here in this country and here in this graveyard I do not know these dead people. I do not know if they lived a good life. Were they bad men? Did they hurt people when they were alive? Is their spirit evil? How do I know their spirit will not kill me? And you? And Mr. Larry?"

I thought about what he had said. I was not a believer but I needed a quick fix to this situation or I'd have to watch the cemetery and him for the rest of the night. I needed to start my patrol and the clock was ticking. I would have to report back soon to dispatch and give them an update.

"Akande, I understand how you feel. We all get scared of the unknown. It's a legitimate fear but I think you'd feel safer knowing that the families of the dead who come here are good, caring people. They would not bury bad people here. It would dishonour their family."

I was bluffing. There was a good chance the cemetery had no less than a few former murderers buried on site but I needed to play on the idea of the love and community in this neighbourhood like he recalled from his village back home. I waved to him to follow me.

We entered the mausoleum and I had him stand on the top step of the stairs leading down to the basement.

"I do not want to go there, Mr. Jaimie."

"You don't have to go down there. I wouldn't do that to you. I can see you're uncomfortable. That's not my intention," I assured him. "I just want you to take a look at what you see down there."

He stared off into the distance and shifted from one foot to the other. "There are flowers and balloons and, I think, vases and candles perhaps?"

"Yes. There are also pictures and letters from loved ones who grieve for their family members. These people who you are afraid of are surrounded by love. They are protected by the people who loved them most in life. Do you think they'd allow evil into this house?" I spread my arms wide and looked up at the ceiling for dramatic effect.

He stood silently for a moment and said nothing. When he finally spoke he asked, "Do the families come here often? Do they pray to Jesus?"

"They do, Akande. Some people stay here all day. Widows weeping over their lost husbands. Some of these people have been buried here a long, long time. Still their families remember them and talk to them through the walls. It's the same out in the cemetery, Akande. Beautiful gardens and angels of every description looking over the spirits of everyone here."

"I understand what you are trying to tell me. My concern is for those who have died with no family to protect them. It is their spirits I fear. Angry in life because they were alone. Angry in death too."

Damn. He wasn't buying it.

"I will sit inside this door when I need to warm up. I will not go down those stairs, Mr. Jaimie. I have my doubts still. But there is a job to do. I do not want to disappoint you or Mr. Larry. I must face my fears tonight I suppose. You have been very patient and understanding. I will not disappoint you."

"Welcome to Beacon Hill, Akande. We serve and protect the dead. The angry spirits need us to keep them in line. We will not be scared."

He nervously half-smiled and probably just a bit anxious that I might be making fun of him. I did no such thing. I was trying to motivate him. At least he wasn't frozen with fear any longer.

"Okay, guard the gate until you're too cold and wet and then come in here to thaw out. You've got a phone you can contact me in the patrol car. I'll come back here the minute you need me."

He shook my hand and walked with me back outside. He headed over to his position by the gate and I saw him yanking on it to ensure it was secure – or more likely checking for an escape route. It was then that it dawned on him that we were locked inside a dark, wet, cemetery. He started shaking again.

I had to go. I needed to report in and rendezvous with Larry in Section 3. And so I did. The process was tedious as I had to get out of the car, open a gate, drive through it, get out of the car, walk back and lock the gate again, drive across the street, get out of the car, open another gate, drive through it, get out of the car, walk back and close it, etc. etc.

It took four major gates to get to Larry in and out through Section 2. He was waiting at the fourth gate in his car. I sidled up beside his car so that our driver windows were parallel.

"Hey, man. Any signs of life?"

He laughed, "Not a thing. Fuck it's dark back there. Why don't they have this section lit? I don't have a spotlight on my car. And my flashlight is useless in the rain."

"I don't think it matters much. Hallowe'en is a wash out. Haven't seen a single kid out all night when I was heading over here."

"Different than last year that's for sure," Larry said.

"Really?"

"Yeah, I was here last year as well with Billy. He trained you I assume?"

"Yep. Good guy."

"Bit of a power pusher if you ask me, but he's damn good at his job. We had a few teenagers climb the main gate last year. Billy found them drinking behind one of the crypts in Section 1. They scattered when he hit the spotlight on them – except the two that were fucking like rabbits on the steps. It was two guys. Billy was traumatized for a week. He walked around for days saying 'Why'd it have to be guys, man? Why? Now I gotta wash my brain out with soap.' Hahahaha."

I wasn't sure if he was a homophobe or not. Either Larry *or* Billy. I just nodded.

My walkie-talkie soon went off. It was Akande – I had given him the walkie-talkie's phone number (it doubled as a radio and a phone).

"Are you okay, Mr. Jaimie? Are you coming by here soon?"

"Yes, Akande. I'm just checking with Larry to make sure he's okay. I'll be there shortly."

Larry wasn't sure what I was talking about.

"Akande's afraid of graveyards," I said to Larry.

He rolled his eyes. "Why would they send him here?"

"I don't know. Maybe he was sent to spy on us and report back to let the big bosses know whether we were kicking back and sleeping."

"Could be. It's gonna be a long, dull night. Sleeping sounds like a great idea."

"I didn't hear that," I said with a smile.

We both turned our cars around in the entrance of the gate – Larry heading back into Section 3, and I back into Section 2 for another game of Open-The-Fucking-Gate/Close-The-Fucking-Gate.

When I got back to Section 1 Akande was standing outside again pacing back and forth in front of the main gates like a tin soldier. He was soaking wet and still shaking. I rolled down my window and shouted.

"Get in the car!"

He walked over to me slowly and I shouted at him again, "Let's get you warmed up."

He got in the passenger side and immediately leaned over to look at the dashboard. "How much gas do you have? What if you run out of gas? They will get you, you know…."

"No one's going to 'get' me," I responded brusquely.

"I could not do what you do. You are a brave man, Mr. Jaimie."

"It's just a job, Akande. I look at the cemetery as a big park with lots of tall stones in it. Nothing more, nothing less."

"You have never run out of gas?"

"No. We fill the cars at the beginning of the shift. The tank never gets below halfway even after driving for 15 hours."

He went quiet after that as I pulled away to do a perimeter check of Section 1. His eyes were nearly popping out of his head from fear. He was like a dog on a road trip that knew he was going to the vet at the end of the journey. There was a nervous excitement but it was tinged with anxiety. He was killing me. I felt so bad for him.

"You really should go home. You can't possibly need money this bad. We're here until 2AM. The subways are going to shut down by then – and you're still a long way from there. You should leave now. Get some warm clothes on and go to bed," I nearly pleaded with him.

"I am not a quitter. I have faced scarier things in my own village. It was so bad I left and went to The Netherlands. I wasn't supposed to be a security man. I was trained to teach."

"Teach what?"

"Mathematics. But it was not to be. The Dutch and African people have a long history of distrust. I came to Canada instead. I was welcomed here but to teach they wanted me to go back to school all over again. I had to make a choice. I needed to work to feed myself and to make money to send back to my family."

"When was this?"

"It has been eighteen years. The company treats me well. I cannot complain and so I will do a job I do not like so that I can continue to help my family."

"Have you ever thought of going back?"

"There are no opportunities there for me and I fear they would not let me leave again. It is a young man's game. Instead, I want to bring my family here. They could have a better life. My son is coming next year."

It hit me then that this was a man who'd already been to hell. He left his home, his family, his entire way of life only to make sure that those who were left behind could reap the benefits of his new freedom. And here he was stuck in a patrol car, with a fat, white, ageing Canadian facing one of the biggest fears of his life: the ghosts of dead people.

The remainder of the night was uneventful. Akande never grew completely comfortable driving through the cemetery. He survived though. I kept him talking the entire time to keep his mind off his fears. I learned a lot from him about the world and his view of it. When the shift was done I offered to drive him to his home. He was most appreciative. I ended up thanking him for his life lessons and for humbling me. He was the bravest guy that night. He could have left and gone home but there was more at stake than his superstitions. People were counting on him. Living people.

TWO MONKS, A WIDOW, AND TWIN CHILDREN OF A MURDERER WALK INTO A BAR

I got a frantic call from Emily at head office one day. She was being over run by several groups of people simultaneously. She was really good at multi-tasking but there were 15 people crowding the waiting area at reception. She needed me to lock the doors and ward off anyone trying to get in after them while she sorted everyone's troubles out.

Two monks were there to ask if they could use the phone to call 911 for an ambulance as one of their fellow worshippers had passed out in a common area of the cemetery for praying. Emily obliged and they sat quietly on a love seat in one corner of the reception area waiting.

Meanwhile, there was a very old Slavic woman sitting on a couch crying with members of her family surrounding her. She was distraught and they couldn't get her to stop crying. She had brought her sons and their wives and some of the kids to arrange services for her husband. Apparently, they'd been married 63 years. Emily had called for a funeral director to come out and walk them through the process.

The last two people were twin Asian women who wanted to know where their mother was buried. They didn't have much information to go on as they'd grown up in Hong Kong after their mother had died here in Canada. They wanted to exhume her remains and take them back to Hong Kong where the remainder of the family had been living for the last 25 years. Emily began the search on her computer database. This is when everything went sideways.

Emily found the record of the mother's burial.

"Oh, yes. Here it is. I'll have to get a director to come talk to you about the exhumation, if it can even be done. Approval will have to be given from the person who paid for the burial as well. It lists a Ky Sun Wong. Do you know this person?"

The twins looked at each other and their faces grew ashen. One of the women spoke up, "That's our father."

"Well, if you can get him to come in and speak with one of our directors we'll see whether we can accommodate your request."

"We don't know where he is. He could be dead but we think he's probably still in jail."

Emily frowned, "That's going to be a problem, I'm afraid."

At that moment the funeral director who was hailed to deal with the Slavic widow and her family happened to hear the conversation.

"Is there anyway you can prove he's dead? Can you find the prison he's in and get him to sign off on this?"

One of the girls started to cry. The other responded, "We were little girls when he killed our mother. We haven't had contact with him since we were four years old and they sent him to jail."

The room went silent except the soft weeping from the Slavic widow who was out of earshot. Then one of her grand children, maybe six or seven years old who'd been pre-occupied with a bottle of water, ran up to where the women were standing, pointed at them and in a sing-song voice yelled out, "Your daddy killed your mommy, your daddy killed your mommy…"

All hell broke loose. The two Asian women burst into tears. The father of the kid scooped up the child and rushed for the door, I quickly unlocked it and let them out. The Slavic widow screamed out and fell on the floor and began rolling around calling out her husband's name as she did.

Emily and the funeral director grabbed the twins and took them into a processing room shutting the door behind them.

At that exact moment the ambulance arrived to assist the two monks who had been sitting quietly and saying nothing. I let the paramedics in and the first thing they saw was the widow rolling around on the floor.

"Is this the call?" One of them asked me.

"No but I'm thinking you might want to take care her first."

And so they did. They took her outside and the other family members followed. She was soon ushered into a black sedan and taken off site by one of her sons. The remainder of the family returned and Emily called in another funeral director to deal with them.

The monks stood up and I introduced them to the paramedics. They hopped in a rather expensive black SUV and the EMS ambulance followed them to the common praying area. As quickly as it had begun the circus broke up. If I hadn't been there I would never have believed any of it.

THE GREAT FLOOD OF 2015

It was another typically quiet Sunday when I was flagged down by some people who were visiting a family grave. They wanted me to know that there was a large pool of water forming around some graves and weren't sure if it was from rain or a broken sprinkler.

I trudged through the grass as one of them took me to the spot. They were a bit distressed as the grave they wanted was now under six inches of water. I called the only maintenance guy on duty, Lopez, and told him what was happening. He drove out from one of the maintenance yards to meet me. We walked around the perimeter of the massive pool. Behind one of the tombstones we could see a small burst of water breaking the surface. He walked through the soggy grass to take a closer look. It was one of the water posts that were located every hundred feet on the grounds that allowed the staff and visitors to hook up hoses and water the grass and flowers. It had clearly been snapped off at the base. Without the faucet acting as a shut-off valve, the water was free to fly everywhere. And it was. Lopez figured one of the seasonal staff had run it over with a lawn mower the day before.

The issue was how to turn it off. We headed back to the maintenance yard and he pulled out some ancient cemetery maps. They had been drawn back in the 1940s when the water system was installed. The newer, automated sprinklers out by the front gates came later and weren't located on these maps. Fortunately, the section we were concerned with was clearly marked as were the shut-off valves. We just had to go find them in the grass. Without knowing which pipe was feeding the water to the broken pipe, we decided to shutdown everything feeding that section of the cemetery.

He handed me a spade. It was going to require digging through sod which tended to grow over everything including grave markers and shut-off valves. The first one was the easiest to find as it was practically in a gutter where the grass and the asphalt met. We pulled the protective cover off the opening. The faucet was damaged and rusty. He threw on a pair of gloves, reached in the hole and turned the faucet. One down.

The next shut-off was near the Beacon Hill entrance gates. It was a lot harder to find. The map showed it in a spot that had been re-landscaped in the 1990s. There was a small hill there now. We poked around in the grass for about 20 minutes in hopes that the landscapers hadn't buried it. We got lucky. In between two burial markers was a similar looking green plastic lid. I popped it open with the spade and Lopez again reached in to turn it off but this time there was no faucet and only a threaded pipe that was once attached to it. He went back to his truck and grabbed a wrench. A really big wrench. It had a weird socket elbow and allowed him to fit it into the confined space of the shut-off box. He was successful. Two down.

He knew exactly where the last shut-off was in another are by a pedestrian walkway. This walkway ran parallel to the trees and halfway down was a brand new ten-foot stone pillar with memorial name plates mounted on all four sides. It was located at one of the many memorial walks and these were the people honoured in this quiet little forest. The pillar looked like one of those old stands you'd buy to put VHS tapes in but it towered over my head and was about five feet wide on all sides. The shut-off valve was inside the monument.

Lopez fiddled with a plaque at about shoulder height and had me hold it. Underneath was an old-fashioned door lock. He pulled out a key and gave it a turn. The entire front of the pillar opened toward him with a compressed air whoosh. It was a secret entrance just like in a horror film! He reached inside and pulled a cord in the ceiling and a light turned on. Below him was a metal ladder. "I'll be back in a minute."

I watched him climb down below ground level and walk away from the ladder. I couldn't see him but he was talking to me the whole time. "The shut-off was moved down here in case of a cataclysmic system failure in the cemetery. There's a redundant one of these rooms near the Section 2 entrance beside the staff building."

He popped back up in a few seconds saying he'd turned off the faucet. He locked the room again and replaced the plaque to where it belonged. "Let's go look at the pool now."

We drove back out to the scene of the water crime. To our dismay the water was still coming out. "This makes no sense," he said.

He pulled out his cellphone and phoned the cemetery manager. If we couldn't shut the water off, the entire section would be flooded by morning. He explained what was going on. I heard a few "uh-huhs" and "okays" and then he put the phone away. "He thinks we need to shut off the redundancy as well. It still makes no sense but we'll have to give it a try or it'll mean calling the city and having them shut off the water to the whole cemetery."

At the Section 2 staff building the shut-off was located under street level as well in an old-fashioned manhole feed. He pulled out a pickaxe from the back of his pick-up truck and jimmied the lid. It tipped up and we rolled it onto the nearby grass. "You're going to have to come down with me. There's no magic light in this one. Just rats."

"Um...what's that now?"

"Don't worry, you can stand on the ladder. The sewage flows below the ladder. You don't want to get your uniform messed up. But I need you to hold a flashlight cause the shut off is about 10 feet down the tunnel."

I'm pretty sure I changed colour. I'd been down a sewer once before back in the 1980s when I worked for the City Works Department. Management there thought us cushy office staff personnel needed to see how the unionized road crews did their jobs and arranged for us to tour a storm tunnel. It wasn't exactly a sewer, but the claustrophobia didn't discriminate.

I grabbed my flashlight and Lopez climbed down the ladder with his trusty wrench. I held my breath, turned around and headed down the ladder backwards. He jumped across the river of sludge and I felt my foot dangling over the last rung of the ladder. I stopped and carefully turned, shining the flashlight his way.

"Point it that way. I'd do it myself but...." I directed to the place where he was pointing his wrench.

"Up a little bit...." I moved the beam.

"Perfect."

I held firm as he cracked open a metal box on the wall. I could hear water running below and distant echoes of something that I really couldn't make out. He started banging on the faucet to get it to move. It appeared to be rusted shut. He applied the wrench. Success! He came back across the sludge trench at my feet. "Alright, if that doesn't work we're fucked."

I climbed back up to the surface and he followed. My shirt had two orange coloured rust stripes down the front. My black pants weren't any better. I tried to brush it off.

"Sorry, man," Lopez said, "Have your company bill Beacon Hill. You shouldn't have to do this bullshit. But thanks for the help."

We drove back to the waterspout. It was a little smaller.

"Hallelujah!!" Lopez yelled, "The pressure stopped so now the system just needs to bleed out. It'll take awhile for the pipes to empty, but it will stop. Hopefully by the end of the day. Make sure you make a note of what we did and leave the report on the site manager's desk. Someone's going to get their ass kicked tomorrow. Time for dinner!"

Lopez ran down to a Filipino restaurant and grabbed us both some food. We spent some time eating and I headed back out to patrol the cemetery once more. People continued to pull me aside to tell me there was a flood for the remainder of the day. I told them we had it under control.

The following day the City had to be called in to shut off the water anyway. We didn't stop the water flow. We'd only slowed it down. The cemetery was without water for nearly a week as they attempted to trace the leak. Turns out the pipe under the section that was leaking had cracked back in the winter and the water had been pooling under the grass since the spring. When the lawnmower tore off the spout and faucet, it released a geyser. It also meant that hundreds of graves located six feet under were probably filled with water. I can't even imagine how the cemetery dealt with that and the families of the deceased.

CHING MING FESTIVAL

The leading cause of angst for me at the cemetery was the Ching Ming Festival. In English that translates as Tomb Sweeping Day and occurs on the first day of the 5th solar term of the Chinese lunar/solar calendar. That usually means 15 days after the Solar Equinox around the 4th or 5th of April. On certain years that also intersects with Christian Easter and holidays from a host of other religions. Ching Ming by itself is unmanageable. Mixing it with other religious observations was cemetery madness.

As I found out Canadian Chinese mourners celebrate Ching Ming twice because some would also recognize the end of summer in late September. So it became a bi-annual celebration for them and nerve-racking mayhem for me. No one told me about any of this when I started at the cemetery. I found out completely by accident that this was even a thing during the second weekend working there.

It was another Sunday with just Lopez and I on site and the skeleton staff dealing with visitations at the V/C. It was beautiful and sunny so the cemetery was full. I didn't realize it was extra full because of what the Chinese families were doing. A few of the roads in and around the three sections of Beacon Hill were impassable. I had to remind many of the people – most not speaking English – that parking on the actual grass wasn't allowed. Those that parked on the road often blocked it. On a good day you could only fit two cars side-by-side on the roads and most of the time you'd have to pull over to let someone pass if both cars were larger than a Prius. Almost without fail people visiting the cemetery drove 1960s Cadillacs or Lincolns. Showboat vehicles.

I got the first glimpse of what was going on when I saw a large congregation of people standing on top of a grave decked out in their Sunday finest. I assumed it was a burial until I noticed there was a full-sized gutted pig on a spit being cooked over an open flame. They were having a pig roast on this person's grave. This didn't seem right. I made a U-turn at the next intersection so I could go back for a second look.

I pulled over and waved to the closest person. A man came over and smiled at me in the window.

"Sir, what's going on here?"

"We are celebrating the life of our father!"

"But you're cooking food. I don't think this is allowed. It's most definitely a health risk."

Just then a tall woman peeked over his shoulder and shoved a paper plate at me. It was covered in fruit, vegetables and a rather large mound of pork.

"Come! Come have some food. There's some for everyone!"

"Um….no, ma'am. I can't take gifts while I'm on duty. I don't mean to disrespect your ancestors but could you make this fast? I'm not sure I'm supposed to let you do this."

I was looking past the duo that was being very hospitable. There were people with plastic cups all commanding a toast.

"Okay, what's in the cups?"

The woman answered, "It's wine!"

"Unfortunately, that is a problem. You can't have open alcohol in here. It's not just a cemetery policy, it's a city wide one."

She frowned and then headed back to the group of revelers shouting something in Mandarin or Cantonese. I looked at the gentleman still standing by my window and said, "Tell you what. I've got to do another patrol around the cemetery but when I come back, I hope to see everything cleaned up and put away."

"No problem, he said. Thanks for understanding."

True to his word, the pig and the spit and all the food were gone. I got back just as the last of the family were getting into vans and heading out. This was a good first encounter. Subsequent encounters would prove to me less friendly.

Conscientious mourners like these people were kind enough to put their fires out, clean up their food, pack up and leave. Others skipped the step involving the putting out of fires. Instead, they'd dump the cinders and ash into nearby garbage containers – which were empty 40 gallon oil drums – and then bugger off. A smoldering pile of cinders in an oil drum full of dried flowers, cardboard and other waste generally took about 20 minutes to ignite. By the time the drum caught fire the culprits were long gone.

Not long after the pig roast incident I got a call from the V/C that someone had spotted a drum fire. It wasn't far from where I already was. I raced over and sure enough there were flames coming out of the top. I quickly looked for a spout and faucet nearby with a garden house. I was in a dry part of the cemetery as it turned out. I had to rush back to the V/C, borrow some water jugs and race back. Of course, the fire was now blasting out of the top of the can like a rocket booster. I tossed the water onto it. Didn't even make a dent. Back I went for more water and another round trying to douse it. Still nothing. It took four trips to get enough water into the can to flood the fire out. I was covered in ash and coughing. This was not in my job description.

I called dispatch to let them know. They seemed unconcerned. "Have the cemetery give you a fire extinguisher".

I went and talked to Lopez.

"You're never going to get approval for one from the site manager. They're afraid that you guys, the security guards, will lose them or never give them back."

The entire year I was at the cemetery nobody would give me a fire extinguisher. I, instead, patrolled every shift with four 10-gallon water jugs in the back seat so that I could douse fires at the time of discovery. If I caught them early enough they were manageable.

Except the ones that weren't in garbage cans. Maintenance stopped emptying garbage cans Friday afternoon. Leaving the next garbage can clearing until Mondays. That meant an entire weekend of people cleaning up gravesites and the Chinese performing Ching Ming. The cans were filled to overflowing by the time Sunday rolled around.

The hot ash and cinders were often dumped on the strewn overflow next to the cans. On one such day I was eating lunch in the Visitation Center kitchen when I got word that there was a fire not far from where I was. My car was parked out back and as I went outside I looked up to see a massive grey cloud of smoke billowing above the trees. I had my water ready in the backseat but as I went to drive away from the building I noticed another fire at the foot of the V/C driveway.

The grass beside a drum was already on fire and it was being blocked by cars parked beside it and their owners had headed off to gravesites unknown. I couldn't get near it with my car. I had to stop in the middle of the road and hand-bomb the jugs of water. Cars started coming toward me and from around the other side of the V/C. As I was fighting the fire cars were beginning to block the entire road. Everyone was stopped dead blocking the mini-intersection and honking their horns. The only way out was around my patrol car. People started yelling at me from their cars to go back and move the patrol car. The fire was still raging. I ignored them and continued pouring water on the fire.

A youngish woman leaped from a car and tried to grab a jug from my hand.

"What the fuck are you doing?"

"Let me pour the water. You move your car, okay?"

I ran back and drove the patrol car up onto the grass to let the mass exodus through. I walked back to where the woman had put the last of the grass fire out for me. I thanked her. As I gathered up the empty jugs and turned to go back to my vehicle I noticed the first car that had been blocking my access. It had been directly beside the grass fire and was now scorched from the front bumper and across the driver and back passenger doors. The paint over the front wheel well was already blistering. That was going to cost some money.

My cellphone rang. It was the receptionist at the Visitation Centre reminding me that the first fire was still raging a little ways away. I got back to my car and returned to the V/C to refill the jugs. I took another route around the cemetery and my access was completely blocked by vehicles again. I was a good quarter mile away from the fire and the smoke plume was getting bigger and bigger. I couldn't get near it.

I phoned Lopez. "Hey, man, there's a massive fire raging in Section 1C. Do you think you can get to it from the maintenance yard? I'm blocked in from all the Ching Ming people and their cars."

"I'll see what I can do," he said. "If not, I'll call the fire department. We shouldn't have to do this shit."

I couldn't agree more. It was a hazard on so many levels. With a cemetery containing so many historic trees I didn't understand why the powers-that-be didn't curb this kind of behaviour but it continued.

I finally got to the spot where Lopez was just putting out the last of the fire in Section 1C. It had not only been a drum on fire, but an entire grave's worth of dead flowers piled beside it. All ripe for kindling. Lopez had brought out a maintenance truck with its own power hose on it. All that was left was smoldering piles of ash.

"Thanks for catching that for me," I said.

"This isn't your job. This has been going on for years and someone's going to get their ass kicked. These cans should be emptied everyday. I spend all day on Sunday emptying them by myself. I can't get to them all before most of them are set on fire. And there needs to be some rules to stop this from happening. The fire department's here every week now."

"I thought Ching Ming was seasonal?"

"It is. Many families continue to come out and perform ceremonies. One week it's Mom & Dad, the next week they bring the kids, the week after that cousins and aunts and uncles and then the grandparents. And because it's so crowded in here people are smart and stagger the visits well into the fall and then again in the summer. It's pretty much all year round now. I've even seen people cooking food in the snow."

I just shook my head. I was already tired of it. I can't imagine how long he'd been fighting this stupidity.

It became more stupid. In the spring the Ching Ming Festival proper was in full effect. There was a massive influx of people the first weekend of April. It was unprecedented. I was lucky to have gotten the weekend off and did Monday through Wednesday that week instead. When I arrived on the Monday morning and did my rounds I checked in with the maintenance crews to ask them how the fires were over the weekend. I wouldn't see the previous day's guard or his report so I had to get an update from staff.

They reported that it was four-alarm stupid as usual. The management had been smart enough to clear the garbage cans on Friday night this time making the potential for fires smaller, but the infernos still managed to pop up. By Sunday Lopez was emptying the 40 gallon drums as fast as he could into a dumpster across from one of the maintenance yards. Unfortunately one or two of them contained smoldering cinders and the dumpster itself caught fire Sunday night. The fire department had already been in twice to hose it down.

The dumpster was in a sand pit so that trucks could just back up and dump stuff into it from a make-shift dock. It was still smoking. "Should I be worried about this?"

"Nah, they basically flooded the bottom of the dumpster."

I could see water seeping out onto the ground around

it turning everything mud. "Okay. Good. Thanks for the update."

I went about my day on patrol and didn't think much of it until 5PM when the crew had gone home and it was time to lock the maintenance building and the yard. After securing the gate I wandered across the road to the dumpster to have a look. It was smoldering and smoking. I was pretty sure more than it had been.

I made note of it in my daily report and went about doing my evening patrol, lockdown and closing of the entire cemetery over the next few hours. Once everything was locked up I went back to the dumpster. Underneath the smoke rising I could see hot embers. I jumped down off the dock and climbed the side of the dumpster to take a look from every side. There was a fire in one corner. The farthest corner from the dock. I grabbed a shovel and begin tossing sand into the dumpster. It seemed to have done the trick. I sat and watched in the dark for a bit. Another flame popped up in a different spot. More sand. More waiting. Another flame. Holy shit. What the hell was going on?

I readily admit that all I know about fires I learned from the TV show '*Emergency*!' and the movie '*Backdraft*'. In other words, I knew nothing. Clearly the fire was above the waterline from the fire department's hosing but below the surface of all the fresh garbage. If I dumped more sand on it that might put it out...or just delay the inevitable. It was getting late and my shift was almost done. I called dispatch.

"This dumpster is about to go up in flames again. Should I call 911?"

"It's up to you."

I returned to the dumpster and dropped as much sand into the thing as I could. I was getting tired. The sand was starting to feel very heavy. I waited 20 minutes and noticed there was no more glowing so I left. I'd clearly done the right thing because the next morning there was no smoke coming out of it. I'm not sure what would have happened if it had continued to burn. The maintenance guys said that they usually just burn themselves out. But who wants a massive dumpster fire burning all night without any supervision?

The whole thing was so avoidable and yet became normalized while I was there. I should never have been put in that position and it was the only time I had a problem with how the cemetery went about its business. In the year since I left I've heard that the 40-gallon drums have been removed and more eco-friendly waste receptacles have been permanently installed. Hats off to them for their eco-efforts and reducing the safety hazards of the Ching Ming celebrants.

CHAPTER NINE

PATROLS

Though opening and closing the cemetery was of chief importance to my duties it wasn't the prime function of the job. Technically the cemetery staff could open and close quite easily and did so prior to the company I worked for being contracted. With the growth of the cemetery along with the neighbourhoods surrounding it security during business hours became paramount. You couldn't have that kind of acreage left unattended while the maintenance staff and funeral staff was trying do their jobs. With an hour and a half dedicated to opening the site in the morning and two and half dedicated to closing and securing it at night that left a whole lot of time for shenanigans. And there was plenty of it.

GRAVESTONE SOUL PICNIC

There are plenty of old century homes by the cemetery, and a few were expropriated back in the day to house staff who lived on site in lieu of a security force. In modern times security and cleaning/janitorial services have been contracted out. In the early days both those jobs were usually foisted on a live-in caretaker. The house he once occupied had long been converted into a storage building – a place to keep extra tents for graveside services, grass cutting gear, signage and wreaths for Remembrance Day and Christmas.

Security's job each shift was to ensure the house was secure, that the ongoing assault of junk mail from Canada Post was cleared and there was nothing amiss on the property. The backyards from the street behind the cemetery shared a fence with the house. It wasn't unusual to find tennis balls or basketballs from kids that had hurled them over the fence and subsequently too afraid to walk into the cemetery to retrieve them. I always threw them back over the fence. I expect the kids appreciated the courtesy.

More times than not there would be raccoons camped out in the backyard of this house or in the carriage house behind it. In the daytime they'd scurry off. At night-time I left them alone especially since they'd shit everywhere and you didn't want to be walking through it.

Imagine my surprise then to wander into the backyard of the house one day only to find three women sunbathing in bikinis, drinking wine and otherwise having themselves a good 'ol picnic. It was a Tuesday. Didn't these people work? The red and white checkered blanket was out and the entire surface was filled with food. It was a beach blanket cliché come to life.

"Ummm….ladies, you can't have a picnic in here. This is private property."

All three of them frowned at the same time. "Ahhhh…."

"Oh, and you might want to go home and take showers. The grass is filled with raccoon poop."

All three looked at each other and jumped up

simultaneously, "Ewwwwwww."

I left them to their own devices knowing they would high tail it out of there in short order.

TEENAGE RAMPAGE

The level at which people seemed to make themselves at home in Beacon Hill was astonishing. In the winter there were people skiing and snow shoeing across the graves. In the summer it was a whole other level of disrespect and daring do.

Concrete abutments and walls and stone benches surround many of the memorial monuments for the very, very rich. Folks often took these as invitations to eat lunch on or sunbathe. I yelled a lot at people doing this. The adults were often embarrassed by their own bad behaviour, but teenagers were a whole other breed. They just didn't give a shit. They made no distinction between a place of silent contemplation and the schoolyard they were heading to or from.

The most common issue was the loitering in and around monuments. On more than one occasion I caught kids trying to break into crypts. Not sure how they thought they would accomplish that as the tombs were usually gated and secured with padlocks. But some idiot always tried. Others believed that the memorial waterfall and reflecting pool was a great place to roll up their pants and run through the water. It was on those days that I'd wish I were dealing with seniors' speed walking at shopping malls instead.

It's interesting to note that despite all their bravado I'd never find them in the mausoleums where the glaring and obvious presence of death would surround them.

The most dangerous thing was that the little bastards liked to set things on fire. Forget bar mitzvahs, apparently coming of age for teenage males in this part of town required being initiated as an arsonist. The first incident had no witnesses. I got a call from Emily at head office letting me know that a jogger reported a tree on fire in Section 2. I raced there and arrived just as some maintenance crews were dousing the blaze. It was a string of trees that had a memorial pathway running down one side. The very first tree in the row was scorched from the ground to about 8 feet up the front. I got back in my patrol car and began scouting the area. There was no one around other than older women attending to some gardens and other folks just arriving in cars to visit their loved ones.

The second event was a week later. One of the site supervisors, Mark, caught two teenaged boys on their way to school trying to light one of the centuries old trees on fire. Animals had hollowed it out over the years and had a very large exposed hole in its trunk around eye level. Idiot Boy #1 and Idiot Boy #2 were attempting to make kindling out of a notebook they had with them. Mark and I escorted them off the property. Mark told them that if they were seen in the cemetery again he'd call the police the next time. I called back to dispatch to add a note in the other security guard mailboxes to be on the lookout for these two kids.

Fast forward about a month later and I get a radio call from Mark, "Remember those kids trying to light that tree on fire?"

"Yeah, are they back?"

"Yep. Section 2, west side this time, near the pedestrian entrance. Can you go deal with them?"

"I'm on it."

I drove over to Section 2 and could see these same two kids, standing in the rain, attempting to light the branch of a very green cedar tree on fire. I started to laugh and crawled slowly up to them in my patrol car. I rolled down the window and just sat watching them from about 10 feet away. They couldn't get the cigarette lighter to work. The rain kept dousing the flame. I broke the silence.

"I'm trying to figure out what's more stupid: that you

would come to a cemetery and try to light a tree on fire in broad daylight, twice, or that you'd come back a third time and try to do it again in the rain. You're not the brightest boys in the school are you?"

The taller of the two dropped the lighter and bolted. The other kid who had his back to me looked over his shoulder and took off behind him screaming as he did. I was immediately struck by the thought that I was going to have to chase these kids, Hollywood movie-style, on foot across the cemetery. I was in no mood to run. I was in no mood to be out in the rain.

I had a better idea. I called Mark and told him to meet me at the street entrance to Section 2. I was going to box them in so their only escape route would be the entrance. First I got out and recovered the cigarette lighter and noticed only then that there were papers on the ground around the tree. They must have tried lighting them first but with the rain making the pages wet the kids abandoned them for a failed attempt at lighting the tree directly. I poured through the three or four pages. One was a quiz and had a student name at the top. The other was a school notification about designated holidays with the school name printed on it. Bingo.

Idiot Boy #1 and Idiot Boy #2 danced and ducked behind tombstones as I weaved along the roads with the patrol car. They were perfectly happy thinking they were baiting me. They had no idea I'd already set a trap at the exit. They also didn't know that I had all day to wait them out. Twelve hours patrolling means there's a lot of time to kill. I was prepared to give them two hours to get over to the gate if I had to. In the end it was 45 minutes.

The Idiot Duo had to leave the safety of the gravestones and the grass and walk on the roadway to get to the entrance/exit. Mark was waiting for them along with a more senior member of the cemetery staff named Helen. When the teens saw this they turned to run and I had already closed the gap behind them with the patrol car –

and then I got out and walked toward them and said, "We're going to ask you to leave. If you return to the cemetery you will be charged with trespassing and arson. We know what school you go to and at least one of your names. This is a friendly warning. The next time will be dealt with by the police."

They had finally gotten the message and ran between Mark and the gate and promptly left. I went out onto the street to see where they went. They were running away as fast as they could. I gave the documents to Mark and explained to the senior supervisor what I'd seen. She asked that I keep her up to date should they come back again. We suspected that this team was responsible for the very first tree fire as well as the one Mark caught them trying to light weeks before. It was a serious situation because the entire cemetery could burn to the ground.

Mark and Helen left and I went inside the staff building beside the entrance gates to wash my hands. While I was in the bathroom I could hear laughter and clearly the voices of two boys. Are you kidding me? The door to the building was 90 degrees to the entrance gate. I opened the door and stood watching. Sure enough the Idiot Boys poked their heads through the pedestrian side of the entrance gate. By then I was already filming them with my cellphone, "Howdy boys."

They jumped a mile when they saw me and ran. Again. What they didn't know was that the staff building had a back door that opened up onto the street outside the cemetery property. I had the key to it and beat them onto the sidewalk. They were looking backward at the gate thinking I was going to chase them. Instead the tallest one slammed into my chest. As he looked up to see what he'd hit I took a picture of his face. He stepped backward and the other kid tried to go around him. I got his picture too.

"Well, boys, these pictures will be emailed this evening to the principal of your school. I expect you'll be punished appropriately. Have a great day."

I expect they shit themselves all the way home. We should have had them arrested but the cemetery wanted no part of any legal issues down the road. Hopefully, the school dealt with these two kids appropriately and they wouldn't be saddled with a juvenile record.

EMERGENCIES

With so many people walking, jogging, and cycling through the cemetery daily there was always the chance that someone would be injured on site. The cemetery attempted to minimize these incidents by forbidding skateboards and roller blades especially in lieu of the massive valley and ravine slope that defined Section 2 and would often attract the users of both. I estimate that I booted out skateboarders once a day during the good weather months.

It was common to have to call EMS paramedics in to deal with dehydrated joggers who had passed out or cyclists who'd taken a spill despite there being not a single pot hole in the entire cemetery. You can't do much about people being their own worst enemies.

Funeral assistants were also prepared with water and first aid kits during graveside services as well. The stress of grief would often lead to older family members fainting either out of shock or the hot weather. I was told that prior to my arrival there as security guard one man had succumbed to a heart attack while standing over the grave of his recently deceased wife. They buried him beside her three days later.

There was also the time that the jilted wife and mistress of a dead man battled it out in long black dresses and high heeled shoes on top of his grave as they were lowering the casket into the grave. They were pounding the crap out of each other and had to be separated by staff with hoses. EMS was called to tend to cuts, abrasions and sprained ankles.

Less common was traffic accidents inside the cemetery.

With miles of roads inside the grounds it's a miracle more people didn't crash into each other. Two major incidents stand out in that regard, though; One involved the T-boning of a cyclist, the other involved mental illness.

THE MINI COOPER GETAWAY

Head office got a call one afternoon that there was an accident just inside the vehicle entrance of Section 2. The call was relayed to me. This was the same entrance where I chased away the teen arsonist. I drove over as quickly as I could and found a woman sprawled on the ground beside her bicycle and a second cyclist who turned out to be her boyfriend standing beside her.

"Is everyone alright?" I asked.

The boyfriend spoke first, "Some woman in a red car came through the gate and cut us off."

The woman on the ground continued, "I slammed into the side of her car. She got out and started yelling at me for putting a dent in the car."

"Did you get her information? Insurance, name, etc.?"

"No. She jumped back in the car and took off. She didn't even ask if I was alright."

"How are you feeling?"

The boyfriend jumped in again answering for her, "She's fine. Her bike's completely wrecked though. Are you going to chase after her? She left the scene of the accident!"

I was getting annoyed. I stepped between him and her and knelt down to see how she was.

"Ma'am, I need you to answer a few questions. I need to assess whether an ambulance should be called."

She nodded.

"What's your name?" She gave me her name.

"Where do you live?" She gave me her address.

"Can you tell me how you hit the vehicle?"

"I got to the gate entrance at the exact same time as the car pulled in. It was a bright red Mini Cooper. I slammed on my brakes and turned but my front tire and handle bar hit the front fender. I was thrown off the bike."

"Did you hit the car with your body?"

"No. I hit the centre post of the handle bar with my stomach. It's really starting to hurt now."

The boyfriend repeated that she was fine. I looked back at the woman and addressed her directly.

"Do you have any other pain? Headache? Neck pain? Numbness? Dizziness? Anything else?"

"No. Just this pain where I hit the handle bars."

"Ma'am, for your own piece of mind and mine I need to call EMS and have them look you over."

The boyfriend was getting impatient.

"How long is this going to take? It's going to start raining soon and I don't want to get stuck out here with our bikes in the rain."

"Well, her safety is my priority. I need to bring an ambulance in. If she refuses help I need both of you to fill out a declaration. I don't recommend it cause the cemetery's lawyers will be ringing your bell. Last thing they want is a lawsuit."

The woman grabbed her boyfriend's arm and pulled herself up. "We need to do this. I feel sick now."

I had her sit on the steps of the staff building beside the gate and gave her some water. I got on the phone and called 911.

They wanted to talk to the cyclist. They asked the same questions I did. I then spoke to the operator again and we compared notes. I requested EMS and a police car. They sent both. When the services arrived I gave the paramedics and the cops a status report. EMS decided they needed to take the woman to the hospital and have some scan done in case there was internal bleeding.

The boyfriend was pissed, "I need to go with her. What am I going to do with the bikes?"

I offered to lock them up in the staff building and gave him my cell number, "Give me a call up until 10PM tonight and you can grab 'em before I lock up for the night. Or if you want to come by tomorrow I'm here from 7AM to 10PM."

He looked relieved and got into the back of the ambulance with his girlfriend.

I turned to the cops, "I think the car that hit this woman is still here. I have a feeling she's one of the regular visitors that comes in a few times a week to visit her family. It's a red Mini Cooper. If you want to follow me I think I know where she is."

We got into our respective vehicles and took off back to the front of Section 2 where the Gothic mausoleum was located. Sure enough, sitting directly in front was a red Mini Cooper. We got out of our cars and approached the vehicle. Right where the cyclist said she'd hit the front fender was a large dent with a crease in it that had peeled back the paint.

I pointed to the mausoleum and said to one of the cops, "She's in there."

The two officers decided to wait it out and returned to their car. It began to rain so I went and sat in my own patrol car beside them. About ten minutes later two more cop cars showed up and an Emergency Task Force vehicle. Now I was concerned. I rolled down my window to talk to the cops.

"What's going on?"

"We ran the plates. This car was involved in another cycling accident last year."

Uh-oh.

The woman came out of the building a few minutes later. A team of cops swarmed her as she attempted to get into her car. She was escorted into the back of a cruiser. I was left in the dark about what was going on until I started to see the other police vehicles start to leave. The two officers that were leading the accident investigation let her out of the cruiser and she got into her car and drove off.

The patrol car window rolled down and I did the same.

"She tells us that she gave the cyclist her driver's license and insurance information before she left the scene. We're heading up to the hospital to see how the cyclist is doing and to question her some more."

"So you can't charge this driver with anything?"

"The problem is that this accident is on private property. The cyclist would have to take civil action against the car driver if she wants to pursue this."

With that I thanked them and said our goodbyes.

The couple did return that night, after the rain had stopped, to collect their bicycles. The woman looked tired but healthy and thanked me for my help. They got stranded for a few hours at the hospital because they had no cash on them. They managed to hitch a ride back to the cemetery with a Good Samaritan. They drove away slowly as the woman's bike was the worse for wear. I'm not sure if any legal action was ever taken concerning the Mini Cooper driver.

SMASH UP DERBY

The other major accident I had to deal with involved a woman who was mentally ill. It was a bright sunny afternoon this time and I was wending my way back to head office to grab my lunch from their kitchen fridge. As I pulled up a passer-by knocked on the patrol car window and pointed to my right, "Someone's smashing their car into other cars in the parking lot."

I spun the wheel and headed over to the employee parking area located between head office and the Visitation Centre. It wasn't an actual parking lot but a strip of roadway reserved for employees to leave their car out of the way of regular traffic in an area that didn't get many visitors. The problem was that a few cars were always parked perpendicular to a T-intersection that connected two access roads with little room to manoeuvre around them if you did need to visit a grave in that section.

On this particular day a driver had failed to negotiate the left-hand turn at the T-intersection and side-swiped an employee's car. As I arrived the driver was backing up trying to get away from the other car, turning the wheel in the wrong direction and then clipped the back bumper of the same car. Problem was this driver kept going, mounted a standing rock that sat on the grass and was now sitting on top of it with their car. As I approached the vehicle, the driver's head was down, focusing on what I assumed was the stick shift and the clutch and kept rocking back and forth on top of this rather large stone.

I knocked on the driver's window. It appeared to be an old woman. She was still transfixed by the stick shift. There was a small yappy dog bouncing back and forth from her lap to the passenger seat. I pounded hard on the window this time and yelled, "Stop the car!!"

No response.

The car was a late model Fiat – one of the pre-Chrysler models, and practically an antique. She was grinding the car into scrap metal. The front bumper was torn off as she reversed, then she punctured the radiator when she drove forward again. I decided to wait it out. The car wasn't going to last much longer. I radioed head office and let them know that there was at least one damaged employee vehicle and to call 911 because I wasn't sure whether this woman was on a suicide mission or having a seizure.

I stood beside my patrol car out of harms way and watched her car slowly screech to a halt. The entire front end of the Fiat was now lying on the ground. The standing stone seemed no worse for wear surprisingly. Two staff members came up beside me including the owner of the car that had been sideswiped and battered. She was understandably upset.

I approached the Fiat. The woman was staring straight ahead, one hand on the steering wheel, the other gripping the dog. I knocked on the window again, "Ma'am, can you open the door?"

She didn't look up. She seemed catatonic. I was getting worried. I tried the door handle. It opened. I kneeled down beside the car so I was eye level to the woman. I waved my hand in front of her face. She didn't react. I carefully placed my hand on the one gripping the steering wheel. It was stone cold. I checked her pulse. It was bottoming out. The dog didn't seem to care. It freed itself from her grip and jumped out of the car. I told one of the staff members to get some water – a dish for the dog and a bottle for this poor woman.

Eventually the woman came around and I began to ask her questions. It was impossible to tell if she was slurring her speech or speaking a different language. Nothing was making sense. We needed to get her out of the car. Fortunately, EMS arrived to do what I couldn't. They attempted to talk to her as well. They managed to wrestle some identification from her purse and gave it to me. She was 78 years old.

Soon a police officer arrived and I gave him a status update. He took the I.D. and headed to the ambulance where the woman was sitting on the back step. The paramedics said she was dehydrated and seemed to be suffering from a medication issue – either too much, or not enough. The cop asked permission to look in her purse further. He found some prescription meds. The paramedics confirmed they were anti-psychotics.

The officer was new to the beat and phoned his supervisor to find out what to do next. The supervisor was in the area and would be on site shortly. The car was going to have to be towed. The woman's driver's license was in a wallet with an Automobile Association membership card. I called it in.

I stood with the officer, the cemetery staff members, and the dog waiting for the police supervisor and the tow truck to materialize. EMS had the woman lying on a stretcher in the ambulance now. She was going to be okay but it would require a trip to the hospital to get her medications balanced again.

The flat bed tow truck arrived and the driver was actually surprised by the wreckage of the cars – both the woman's battering ram and the staff car that had been strafed. He put the Fiat on the hoist and loaded it onto the flatbed. It was there, standing at eye level to the car that I noticed something odd. I called the policeman over.

"Look at the side and the back of this car. It doesn't match the damage from the rock or where it scraped the red sedan. The opposite side of this car has grey paint all over it and the tail light is gone."

As if someone had been listening to our conversation the cop's radio went off. It was his supervisor. He grabbed the call and walked away from where we were standing. I could see him shaking his head. When he came back he looked shocked.

"My supervisor's hung up with another issue, he can't get here for another hour. It seems that before this woman started playing smash up derby here she'd been playing bumper cars on the way from her house to the cemetery. Someone got a plate number that matches this vehicle. There's at least twenty cars with some kind of damage on her street alone."

"Well, that explains the grey paint and the damaged tail light. This woman shouldn't be driving at all. Anything you guys can do?"

"We can file a recommendation to the Ministry to have her license reviewed, but ultimately this rests on her doctors. They need to look at the feasibility of someone this old driving and using anti-psychotic drugs. It's a deadly combination. She's lucky only cars were banged up today."

The paramedics wanted to move her to the hospital. They couldn't take the dog. The car was heading to impound. By this point the cemetery general manager was out and recognized the woman as a regular who came weekly to visit her husband's grave. He was sure there was contact information for the family. He took the dog to his office and made arrangements for her daughter to come pick it up. At last report the woman was back on her proper meds and no longer able to terrorize anyone behind the wheel of a car.

HELPING THE DISTRESSED

The problem with security guard training is that it only covers CPR, First Aid and hazardous workplace safety issues. There was many a day that the floor of a mausoleum was wet from the rain leaking in which I was required to cordon off and secure or that an entire building was filled with killer bees and I could request someone from pest control to handle it.

What they don't train you for is the inevitable showdown with someone not in control of their own behaviour. I could go on at length how society, and governments, have failed the mentally ill. We've abandoned them to their own devices leaving so many homeless and vulnerable.

For whatever reason cemeteries – and Beacon Hill was no exception – drew them in like flies. The straight-up homeless person was easy to regulate. I'd occasionally get one guy with two shopping carts trundle through the property. He was harmless and he'd crash underneath a large tree to escape the heat. He bothered only the elitist, uptight neighbourhood wives of doctors and lawyers or more to the reality of the situation they believed his presence was bothering them. He wasn't harming a soul. I'd often grab a coffee from head office to give to him. He seemed appreciative. Management always forced him to leave though. Wouldn't want to upset those rich joggers. Sometimes I'd see him sleeping in bus shelters on my way in to work. Freezing in the cold. It was heartbreaking.

There were others who were a direct threat though. As usual, I got a call from Mark saying that there was a woman screaming at the traffic coming into the cemetery in Section 3. I drove out to meet him there. He was anxious because the woman wasn't actually in the cemetery. She was standing on the city sidewalk berating visitors as they entered the grounds. Mark tried to reason with her. She began to scream like she was being stabbed. I tried to talk to her. She did the same thing. Then she sat down on the sidewalk and yelled at people walking past and making rude comments and gestures.

Sitting turned into lying down and that turned into her rolling around like a puppy in the grass. The problem was technically out of our hands, but Mark and I aren't assholes. This woman needed help. I called 911 and explained that this woman was clearly in mental distress. They asked if they should dispatch a mental health team. I said yes.

And so they did. No guns drawn, no showdown, no tazering. It was a well-prepared team of trained police professionals listening and talking to the woman to understand her needs and gain her trust. She didn't really believe them, but because they seemed empathetic she reluctantly agreed to go with them. Of course that didn't stop her from yelling profanities as they put her in the back seat of a patrol car. The team got a report from Mark and I and took the woman to a hospital where she could have her symptoms treated.

Not all incidents end as easily.

I was sitting eating lunch in my car one afternoon near the front gate of Section 1 watching people come and go. It was an unusually busy day and several graveside services were planned over the course of the day. I hovered at the front gates in case people needed directions as was frequently the case. This also meant foot traffic. Not everyone arrived in a car as there was bus service directly to the cemetery from a nearby subway stop which is why a woman standing near a rather ostentatious eyesore of a monument dedicated to a captain of industry didn't seem unusual. At first.

Then she started climbing up the monument and began beating a number of brass gargoyles and cherubs with her purse and yelling at the inanimate objects in a Jamaican patois. I dropped my food and got out of the patrol car and approached her.

"Hey! Get off there."

She looked right at me and continued smacking the brass statues. I walked closer. She climbed to the other side of the monument. I followed at ground level looking up at her and telling her to get down like I was scolding a child in a playground. I think she was swearing at me. I took a step forward which she took as a threat and she jumped down and started running.

She looked back yelling at me the whole time. She passed my patrol car and headed toward the gates. Good, I thought. She's leaving. But as she took her first step outside the gate onto the sidewalk a police motorcycle pulled up. It was leading a funeral procession into the cemetery. It nearly hit her, she dashed sideways to avoid it and ran into the middle of Beacon Hill Road. I was running toward the scene at this point. The road was a mass of traffic congestion all hours of the day. She was going to get hit. The cop dismounted from the bike as he would in directing vehicles into the cemetery.

By now she was lying down on the yellow line in the centre of Beacon Hill Road. Cars were swerving and beeping. Traffic was already stopped behind the cop as he had directed them to. He moved into the roadway and stood beside the woman who was yelling and carrying on and he signaled for traffic coming at them to stop. I ran to his side. We both grabbed one of the woman's arms each and dragged her back to the sidewalk. A second motorcycle cop from the back of the funeral procession had seen the commotion and raced up with his lights and siren going to assist.

I was instructed to direct the procession into the cemetery while they dealt with the woman. The two motorcycle cops had to restrain her as she began kicking and screaming. A cruiser was called in to remove her from the site. The mental health unit was not with them. I have no idea how it panned out for the poor woman. I hope she got help.

THE IRISH (A)WAKE

Most interactions were harmless, sometimes even comical. I got a call one day from the general manager running events at the Gothic mausoleum. He had a wedding service coming in for 1PM and when he arrived to start setting up for the event noticed there was someone in the chapel sleeping under the pews. He wanted me to kick the guy out.

When I got there we both went into the chapel and looked down to see a pair of feet jutting out from under a row of pews. I followed them up the row and located the person they belonged to. I had the GM help me lift and move the pew where the guy's head was. I kneeled down and shook one shoulder of the slumbering, snoring, redheaded man. He was on his back and opened one eye. Then the other. He went to move his hands and smacked them on the bottom of the other pews he was wedged under.

"Rise and shine, chief," I said very loudly.

He winced and tried to roll over. Like a barracks gutter crawl he snaked his way out from underneath the remaining pews mumbling to himself. He attempted to stand and had to brace himself against one of the pews. He was hammered.

When he spoke it was the epitome of a ridiculous Lucky Charms cereal commercial come to life. Lots of 'hoity toity' and 'wee bit o' this and wee bit o' that' folksiness. He was very concerned about what time it was.

"It's 12:30, chief. Time for lunch."

"No, it can't be. I was just resting my eyes," he said as he stroked his hair and pulled on his shirt.

"It's 12:30. You clearly slept the morning away. Come on with me outside. You'll feel better in the fresh air."

He staggered beside me and we walked out to the top steps of the mausoleum entrance.

"There ya go. No harm done."

"I can't believe it's 12:30. I need to get me some lunch."

He made it down the steps holding the handrail but just barely. I watched him wander off in a zigzag fashion toward another part of the cemetery.

I found him passed out on a bench an hour later. I let him sleep it off. An hour after that he was gone. He probably left in search of another cup of cheer.

THE REGULARS

It wasn't all high drama. I became friendly with many of the regular visitors. They were my eyes and ears on the ground and I was grateful. I always looked forward to seeing them as well because it meant things were right in their world.

In Section 1 was the multiple dog walker. She came shortly after the gates opened in the morning and had six dogs of various shapes and breeds. Her presence was a constant bone of contention with other regulars because the idea of having a dog in a cemetery was still a hot topic of debate. Bringing six dogs into the cemetery, according to them, was unmanageable. This woman was not only respectful of the rules in the cemetery but so were the dogs. They weren't allowed on the grass and when they did their business she was quick to clean it off the pavement – including hosing it down with the faucet hoses found around the cemetery.

One visitor had it out with her one day. The grounds' supervisor, Mark, and myself were called in to set the gentleman straight. He verbally assaulted the woman and threatened to run the dogs over with his truck. We had him banned from the cemetery.

There was also a gay couple who came through with two giant Great Danes. The dogs would walk past my car and I would only see their legs and underbellies. They were as tall as the patrol car. No one ever hassled with the couple.

Not all the dog walkers were as courteous. I was frequently called to Section 2 to deal with a woman named Alice in her late '70s whose visit every day began with an unsupervised wild run by her black Labrador Retriever named Beowulf. The dog was built like a truck and clumsy, and because she was a frail old thing she literally gave up trying to control the animal. We'd make her track the beast down, put it on a leash and then kick her out of the cemetery at least once a week. It wasn't until much later I was told that this woman was actually suffering from dementia and really had no concept of what the cemetery actually was. We cut her some slack.

Nosy Nancy – the resident busy body and town gossip, relayed this info to me. Her house backed onto the cemetery. She was 86 and had lived there her entire life. Her brother was killed and interred in the cemetery during World War II. She had been coming to visit since 1943 when she was 14. Seventy-two years she'd been coming into the cemetery. According to her calculations she figured she'd spent 68 years there keeping an eye on everything.

She'd gone through generations of workers in the cemetery and its staff. She knew the regulars and the troublemakers. The woman with the dog Beowulf was on her naughty list, "They should never have let dogs into the cemetery. It's disrespectful. I've talked to the Board of Directors about it. They think I'm a nuisance. I can show them where all the dog shit is!!"

I always had to suppress a laugh when she swore because it just seemed so out of character for someone her age. I grew worried for her in the weeks leading up to my quitting the job, though, as she was visiting the cemetery less and less. Turns out she was getting her wrists operated on for carpal tunnel syndrome. She was having difficulty navigating with her walker so on those days I'd throw it the trunk of the car and drive her over to her brother's grave. What was most distressing is that it was a good mile from where she lived beyond the cemetery. She told me that back when he was buried that access from her house to his grave was a direct bee-line but over the years development in the area and the re-landscaping of the cemetery meant she had to walk around the valley. With her walker it was impossible because of the hills going back and forth and she didn't get over to see her brother as frequently as she used to.

Another regular who avoided Nosy Nancy was a semi-retired pensioner named Slim. He seemed rather lonely and only came to the cemetery to eat lunch and feed the squirrels. He'd grown fond of my fellow security officer Billy so when I saw Slim he always asked how Billy was doing and then he'd pull something out of a plastic bag he'd just bought at the nearby grocery store. Usually it was donuts. He'd hand me the box and tell me to share the donuts with Billy. I'd graciously accept and take them back to our security office at the end of the shift to share with anyone left on duty. The remainder would go into Billy's locker for whenever his next shift was. Slim was a great guy and he just wanted someone to talk to, I think. Occasionally I'd pull up a bench with him and we'd have a coffee which, if you know my dislike of coffee, was a bold move.

The two people that always brightened my day were an old couple that stayed strictly inside Section 3. Billy introduced me to them on my first day of training. The woman, Alana, was in her late '60s and in really good health. You could tell that when she was younger she was probably a really attractive and sexy woman. She loved to talk and had a wonderful Eastern European accent.

Her compatriot, as it turned out, was someone she had

met in the cemetery during the times she was mourning her late husband. Arturo was in his early '70s and spoke no English but he and Alana shared a European heritage and grew a strong bond as widow and widower. He clearly adored her and they either walked or rode bicycles through the cemetery every day. Arturo didn't like her talking to us security guards. He didn't know what she was telling us and was sure that Billy was flirting with her.

Turns out as time went on I earned the trust of not just the couple, but Arturo specifically. I never stopped to gossip with her but I made it clear I wanted to say hello to them both. One day I saw him sitting alone on a bench with his bicycle beside him. He had grown tired and Alana toured the cemetery on her bike without him. I pulled my car up to him and rolled down the window and said, "Hello, Arturo, I hope you have a great day."

I watched as the corners of his whiplash moustache curled up on each side of his mouth revealing a beautiful set of white teeth as he smiled. In his best broken English he said, "Great day!"

My next encounter was meeting Alana on her own as she was cycling around Section 3 by herself. She stopped beside my patrol car when she spotted me.

"What did you say to Arturo? He doesn't stop talking about you."

"I just told him to have a great day last time I saw him."

"I can never get him to talk, never mind in English."

"Hey, guess I've got the gift!"

From then on Arturo went out of his way to say hello to me, his English improving progressively over the months. I would add a few words to each dialogue and he'd try things out, never sure if he was making any sense. I reassured him his speech was great. And it was.

The very last encounter I had with the couple was the day I saw them sitting side-by-side on a bench taking a break from their cycling. Arturo was sitting thoughtfully taking in the surroundings while Alana was eating an apple.

As I pulled up in my patrol car I rolled down the window and yelled at Arturo, "Kiss her!"

Alana was not amused and tried to throw her apple at me. She missed by a mile and I started to laugh. As I drove off Arturo laughed and yelled out, "It's a great kissing day!!"

CHAPTER TEN

CLOSING TIME

My duties were elsewhere on nights when there were services at the Visitation Centre because they had plenty of staff to handle most encounters. I spent my time doing the closing procedures – which were the opening procedures in reverse - but had far more time to do it. With the maintenance staff mostly done by 4:30 PM, I was able to go to each building and secure them as needed. The staff was usually great in locking their vehicles and putting the keys away. But occasionally I'd find a truck window open or keys still in the ignition. I was responsible for securing those trucks and tractors and making sure that the keys were put inside where the workers could access them immediately upon arrival each morning.

Most of the lawn equipment and shuttle buses (Trojan-like golf carts were often used to transport summer students or large funeral parties all over the cemetery en masse) were already parked inside the maintenance garages. In an entire year I never found one left outside by accident. These guys were thorough. With that my only job was to make sure the garage doors were closed and locked which was not always an easy task especially if the garage doors were 20 feet tall and the rope to pull them down was tangled…or missing altogether.

I had to then check the upstairs kitchen, change rooms and bathrooms for any irregularities like windows left open or food not properly disposed of. Cleaning staff was ultimately responsible, but by doing my security sweep I could then verify that if anything went hinky later then it could have only been cleaning staff. And good thing too, because they often dropped the ball mostly because they took on too many contracts and never spent enough time in one building long enough to satisfy the conditions of their contract. The floors would still be dirty, or they didn't finish the bathrooms or whatever. Turn over was high and that was problematic in itself as I was often the guy responsible for confiscating their keys to the cemetery once they'd been fired or relieved of duty.

With the maintenance buildings secured and all the internal lights off the alarms needed to be set. That's pretty easy in the summer when it's still daylight out, but wandering around and crawling over machinery to get to an exit in the dark on a winter's night was cause for more than one injured shin on my part. I think I wrecked two pair of pants in a year just smashing into the tow hooks on large ATV's known as Gators. "Hi, I'm the security guard here and I'd like to introduce you to my bleeding leg…"

With the buildings locked down next came the access gates into the maintenance areas from the cemetery proper. I was told that there'd been some theft of equipment in the past so it was imperative that the facilities be chained and padlocked. The exception was the maintenance building closest to the Gothic mausoleum. That building was in a restricted area where the public wasn't allowed at all so there was no gate. However, the public never paid much attention to the "Do Not Enter" signs and the occasional homeless person would find their way back there looking for food and shelter in the garbage bins. I'd usually find raccoons first, but there was the rare occasion where I'd find a person. And we would both be scared shitless.

NONA & THE SANDBOX

Most of the maintenance buildings featured a dumpster for waste, an area to park and store vehicles, and a host of materials required for maintaining graves and gardens. There were designated individual storage units of gravel, sand, compost, topsoil, sod and even trays of pre-potted flowers. These materials aren't cheap and are kept inside the maintenance yard behind a locked gate to prevent poachers when staff isn't on site.

It was my job to secure those gates immediately after the ground crews left for the day. On one particular day I arrived at one of the bigger maintenance yards to find a car inside the gates with a woman and child still in it.

I pulled my patrol car beside the visitor's car and got out and tapped on the window. The driver, a younger woman, pointed behind me. There, walking toward me with a bow legged gate, was an elderly woman about 5 feet tall in a fancy black dress carrying a large yellow bucket full of something. She looked to be in her mid-to-late '70s with short grey hair. She was the epitome of an Italian widowed grandmother.

I approached her and said, "Ma'am, you can't take anything from this yard."

She looked up at me with a smile and said in a thick Italian accent, "It's okay. I know the men here. They said I could take the sand for my husband."

I didn't doubt that her husband was buried somewhere in the cemetery but I didn't believe that the maintenance crew gave her permission to take the materials. The woman in the car was fidgeting.

The old woman waved a hand and yelled at her, "Open the trunk!"

She walked passed me and over to the trunk of the car.

"Ma'am, I don't care who you talked to you can't take anything from here."

"No? I no take the sand?"

I looked in the bucket and laughed, "Ma'am, that's not sand. That's compost."

"Compost? What is compost?"

"It's manure, Ma'am. Horse poop."

She stuck her hand in the bucket, pulled out a hand full of the dark soil and sniffed it. She spit on it and threw it to the ground, then turned the bucket over, dumping the contents at my feet.

"Where is the sand?" she asked me as she pushed past and headed to the piles of gravel and sand.

"Ma'am, you can't take the sand. It belongs to the cemetery."

Just then the woman in the car took off with the trunk still up. She drove straight through the gates and out into the cemetery proper.

The old woman came trotting back and raised her fist and said, "You fuckink (sic) coward. Come back!"

She looked at me again and said, "Pfft. My daughter. She thinks you're going to rape her. She's a chicken shit!"

Without missing a beat she grabbed my arm and said, "Come show me the sand. I need sand."

"Ma'am, you can't take the sand!"

"No?"

"No. And whose bucket is that?"

"Oh, it's yours."

She dropped it on the ground and walked past me out through the large gates waving her fist and yelling, I assumed, at her daughter, "Come back you stupid bitch. I'm a kick your ass. You no leave me here with this man. When you come back I'ma get him to rape you!"

I actually burst out laughing and then locked the gate

behind her.

But the story doesn't end there with this firebrand. She still had one more trick up her sleeve.

NONA & THE CHRISTMAS WREATH

The secretary at head office, Emily, always finished her shift around 4:30PM and I was asked by management to give her a ride to the farthest exit gates so she could catch transit as she lived on the other side of the city. It made her long day a bit shorter and I was happy to oblige.

It was getting colder as we moved into December and she appreciated not having to walk to transit. On one particular day when I was delivering her to her destination we got talking about her day and she was telling me it was a particularly hectic season because the cemetery gave families the option of buying wreaths to be placed on graves. You could pre-order them and pick them up at the office. Emily was in charge of dispensing the wreaths but she noticed on this day that someone had come in to get one and because she was so busy told the woman to help herself to the wreaths sitting outside the front door of the office.

Emily was walking past a window to help another customer and noticed this woman had grabbed three wreaths and ran off down the sidewalk. She asked me if I could keep my eye out for this woman who was small, and about 70-ish years old wearing a fur coat. I said I'd prowl around and see if I could spot her and/or the wreaths.

After dropping Emily at her gate I swung back around to start patrolling again. No sooner had I made it back to Section 2 then I was intercepted by a black SUV coming in the opposite direction with the driver waving at me. I pulled over and the SUV stopped immediately in front of my patrol car. A rather large, imposing woman got out and came over to talk to me. She stuck her head in my window.

"I'm lost. I'm looking for my aunt's grave so I can place a wreath on it. I got this map from the office but I'm not sure which direction I'm facing."

The map had been marked up and notarized by Emily with the location of the grave.

"Oh, you're in the right area. Go back the way you came and the plot will be on you right-hand side. It's going to be about five graves in. You'll have to walk a bit and the grave may not have a headstone…it might be a flat foot stone."

The woman went to say something in response and she was pulled back from the window by two little hands on each shoulder. There, standing behind this woman, was the person I had affectionately called Nona from the sand incident in the summer.

"Don't talk to him. He's a gonna rape you!"

The woman looked at her like she had two heads.

"What are you talking about Mama? This man's giving us directions!"

"He doesn't know shit. I know where my sister is buried. She is over that way," and the old woman pointed in the completely opposite direction to the map.

I signaled to the younger woman to come back to the window as I could see the old woman stomping away yelling something in Italian as she got back in the SUV.

"Say, did your mother happen to grab three wreaths from the office this afternoon?"

"No. Just two wreaths. One for my aunt's grave. One for my father."

"I don't want to accuse her of anything but can you check to see if there's actually three?"

"Um…sure. Hold on."

The woman made a beeline back to the SUV and threw open a back door. I saw her reach in and pull out the wreaths. She stopped to count them and shook her head. She kept one in her hand, threw two back into the truck and slammed the door shut. She then pulled open the passenger door and began berating her mother. It was all in Italian and very heated. Then the old woman reached out. I thought it was to close the door but instead she grabbed the wreath out of her daughter's hands and threw it behind her onto the grass. Then she shut the door and locked herself inside.

The younger woman retrieved the wreath and walked back to me.

"I am so sorry, sir. My mother is out of control. She steals things. I don't know what to do."

"It's okay. We've actually met before. Do you have another sister perhaps? Because there was a similar incident in the summer involving her stealing sand. She was trying to sneak it out in a grey car. Fortunately, I put a stop to it."

"Oh, my God, yes. This keeps happening. We don't know what to do. You aren't going to arrest her are you?"

"No. No. No. I don't have the authority to do that. But your mother is pretty harmless. A pitbull with a big bark and a little bite, but harmless. Please just keep an eye on her. I wouldn't want her to be banned from the cemetery."

"This place upsets her. I don't know why she insists on coming. She just stands at my father's grave and yells at him. She's never forgiven him for dying or her sister who we just lost."

"My condolences. It can't be easy, I'm sure. You're a good daughter. Don't be too hard on her. She's clearly still grieving."

"He died 39 years ago. She should be over it by now but we Italians are stubborn in our traditions. Do you know she has fourteen black dresses? And they're all different. But she wears tan coloured shoes with them. It's embarrassing."

I had to suppress a laugh. The woman could see I wanted to and started to laugh as well.

"Oh, I've kept you long enough. Wish me luck and you have a good holiday. I don't envy you your job dealing with crazy old ladies all day long."

"They make my days interesting. Take care of your

Mom. She needs you."

With that she returned to the SUV and the old woman wouldn't let her in. The daughter used the remote keytag to let herself in. The old woman locked her out again. The daughter pounded on the window and shouted, "Mama, when I get in there I'm gonna kill you."

And so it went. I drove back to head office and dropped off the stolen wreath with a note for Emily.

"Nona says sorry."

MAUSOLEUM PROCEDURES

With the maintenance yards closed the mausoleums were next. Unlike the cemetery itself that needed to remain open until at least sundown, the mausoleums could be cleared, secured and locked down anytime after staff had left the grounds. Some families would arrive late and bitch about not getting access but I was a reasonable guy. It wasn't like the mausoleums had hundreds of people in them all day long. It was usually small families or individuals just wanting to drop off flowers (or those damnable candles) and pay their respects. I gave them time and space to do both and usually did other duties and circled back to lock up behind them. Most were grateful.

A mausoleum in the dark is as scary as it sounds. It's a giant house of horrors if you let your mind get away from you. You move from hallway to hallway turning lights off until you get back to the entrance where you set an alarm and then run for your life to get the doors locked before the motion detectors went off. Worse still was leaving the building, driving past it in the patrol car later and noticing a light still on in a hallway. A light you know you turned off. That maintenance building behind the Gothic mausoleum had the same problem. Despite double-checking the lights every night during lock down, the kitchen light in the maintenance building would always come back on. Some of the cemetery and cleaning staff believe it's where the only known ghost on the site is located. I have no opinion one way or the other.

THE GATES FROM HELL

The remainder of the night would be spent cruising in the cemetery as the night drew on and the sun began to disappear. At this point the gates needed to be systematically closed, with the goal of corralling visitors and pushing them toward specific exits. Those access ways would be closed last. The farthest point in Section 3 needed to be closed first. It was in the quietest part of the cemetery away from the offices and the bustle from main thoroughfares like Johanson Road or Grangley Boulevard. Craymore was a pedestrian entrance only and it led to and from a residential subdivision. A previous manager at Beacon Hill used to leave the gate open as there was an outcry from the citizens that they wanted access to get to a nearby plaza containing a beer store. After several attacks and robberies in and around the area, that idea was scuttled. Locking that gate and its opposite counterpart was priority number one.

Technically, if anyone wanted to get into the cemetery bad enough they'd find a way. But the wrought iron fences are well over seven feet tall so unless you're a pole-vaulter or have someone tag-teaming with you getting over the fence without impaling yourself on the baroque floral spikes across the top was unlikely. The most likely access point is the gate itself but we chained and padlocked those as soon as we were able. Of course, once or twice every night I'd lock a gate and have someone show up behind me wanting out. Those issues were easy while you were standing there. As the night progressed and each of the 51 access points was secured, chained and locked more and more people would be looking for an exit.

Every gate has a sign indicating hours of operation. No one read the signs. Once the sun was down it became a massive game of whack-a-mole. I would race around in the dark in my patrol car with the spotlight on looking for stragglers; people who either got lost, distracted or deliberately avoided me to hang out just a little longer amongst the dead.

It was a bizarre ritual especially when I'd catch young women wandering aimlessly alone in there. It defied logic. Attacks in cemeteries do happen. It's part of the reason why there are now cemetery cops. It's why I was there. The bad shit in the day was easily manageable because there was so many eyes on the ground in the daylight. But at night? It was just me, a walkie-talkie and a car with a spotlight. It was dangerous for anyone after sundown whether she was familiar with the place or not.

I was seconds away from driving off the property one night when I saw a woman running full steam toward me across Beacon Hill Road inside Section 2 of the cemetery. She had her high heel shoes in her hands. I only saw her because my spotlight was still on. I ran across the street and opened the gate to let her out. Had I left she would have had to walk a quarter mile toward Section 3 and use the emergency dispatch phone. A mobile security supervisor on night shift would have had to get her out. She told me she didn't know the cemetery was closing. I asked her what part of pitch black did she not notice?

I tried not to scold people, but there was always that one person who was cocky and just a little too eager to test my patience especially cyclists that I could spot coming in one entrance while I was locking up another one knowing very well it was closing time. Those people I'd chase with the patrol car. I knew more roadways than they did. And I knew them in the dark. It was often a deer in the headlights end game when I would beat them to the next entrance and blast them with the floodlight. Hard to be a smartass when you're blinded and disoriented.

"Oh, I didn't know you were closing."

You just wanted to bitch slap some of them. But I was polite and put on a "I'm-only-making-$10.50-an-hour-at-this-McJob" smile and bid them a good night. Wal-Mart greeters eat your heart out.

Of course, the worst gate in the entire place to close was the ravine gate. Aside from the coy-wolves and deer, joggers would shortcut through the cemetery to hit the trail below. There was an endless staircase leading down to the water, and a footbridge that then connected with another set of trails out into the valley. As previously mentioned access to the gate was at the end of a cul-de-sac for the patrol car and then a 50ft. pathway down to the gate itself. It was on a steep incline. You prayed that the weather was good on the nights you were on duty because the path was either knee deep in snow or ankle deep in mud. Good weather meant an easy time up and down the hill and you wanted to get that gate closed before the sun went down because there was no way of knowing what was going to come up from the valley. Friend, foe or beast. To make sure the closing went smoothly the patrol car needed to be driven onto the first few feet of the pathway so that the headlights and the searchlight illuminated the bottom of the path where the gate was. I never drove too far in. Billy, my security trainer, told me stories of guys having cars slide down the path and into the gate itself. No thanks. I took my chances with my own irrational fear of what might jump out of the valley at me rather than lose a patrol car. The worst that ever came at me was spiders descending from trees blocking my route back to the car.

And so the struggle continued almost to the end of my shift. Chasing people out of gates and locking up behind them. Most nights they allowed me to relax and do my shift reports before I got to secure the main office, closing the main gates and heading off site. That's if the Visitation Centre staff also got finished on time. It was an endless dance of timing. After 15 hours in a patrol car another minute seemed like a life-time.

THE COOKIE GAMBIT
Some interactions start off seriously on the wrong foot.

There were days when I was tired and wanted nothing more than to go home. Getting the buildings secured and the gates locked was mission one and sometimes I got lucky with no one trapped inside the cemetery or any hassles at all. After performing what we called a 'fake lock' to the front gates – where I'd close them but not secure the padlock in case they had to be opened to let out cleaning or admin staff - I'd sit in front of them in my patrol car facing the cemetery head office and just filled out reports while listening to the radio.

Other times I'd spy stragglers off in the distance as a headlight bounced off a grave stone or monument and I'd have to go meet up with them usually because they were lost and I'd managed to miss them because we had been travelling around the cemetery in the opposite direction from each other. During such a night I found a guy who hadn't noticed it was closing time and got disoriented. I asked him to follow me out to the gates. As I pulled up I could see one of the two gates had been opened. The padlock and chain were on the ground. I pulled over and directed the driver out and 'fake locked' the gate again. Someone had sneaked into the cemetery.

There was a small hill near the head office and I moved the patrol car to the top and got out to have a look around. Off in the distance to my right I could see the taillights of a car. Off I went to track down the culprit pulling up right behind them. There was a woman standing about ten feet in on the grass near a grave. I shouted to her.

"Ma'am, the cemetery is closed."

She didn't turn around and yelled over her shoulder, "The gate was open."

"No, it was closed. You jimmied the lock...I found the chain on the ground."

She had turned around to face me, "I need to see my husband. Why are you being a jerk? Why don't you get a job you like if you hate this one?"

Ah, yes. The abusive, privileged self-righteous ass.

"Ma'am, the cemetery closes at 8PM. It's now 8:30PM."

Feigning ignorance she said, "I didn't know what time the cemetery closes."

"Really? How long has your husband been buried here?"

She had now crossed her arms and was starting to fume, "Three years!"

"And you don't know when the cemetery closes? I need you to leave."

"I'm not going anywhere until I've visited my husband."

"I'm calling the police. You're now trespassing and refusing to leave.

"Go ahead, my brother's a cop. He'll kick your ass."

This was becoming an argument of who-could-threaten-who. I counted to three, took a deep breath and gave her a small victory as leverage.

"You have until 8:59PM to get to the front gate. At 9PM the police will escort you off site."

"I'm not going anywhere. I have the right to visit my husband."

She had called my bluff. I didn't want to call the police on something as ridiculous as kicking out a widow.

Thinking over this heated conversation I notice she had two restless children around 8 or 9 years old in the back of her car acting up and yelling.

"I think we got off to a bad start here. I really would like to go home. It's the end of a 15-hour shift for me and I'm sure you'd like to get your kids out of here before the sun goes down completely. Tell you what I'm going to leave these cookies right here…"

I said the last three words very loudly so the kids could hear me. I took two cookies from my knapsack and placed them on the hood of her car and then got in my car and left the graveside. As I drove away I could hear the kids losing their minds even more. I headed straight back to the entrance gates. Five minutes later the woman pulled up to the gates to exit and rolled down her window. I could see the kids gorging themselves on the cookies.

"Well, played."

"Sorry about the loss of your husband. You have a good night, ma'am."

TRAGEDY CAME KNOCKING

Sometimes the complete opposite of having people locked inside the cemetery were those that desperately needed to get in after I'd already locked up. We place an undo stress on ourselves with the construct of time. Calendars and dates become chains to some people and so it came to pass many times that families who absolutely had to see their loved ones on the death date of their deaths needed access to the cemetery even when it was closed.

I was given clear instructions by my employer and by the cemetery that the closing time of the gates was set in stone. If I didn't manage to get to a gate on time and someone sneaked in I was solely responsible for the safety of that person. If they got hurt the liability was on the cemetery, my employer and me. I did not want that type of responsibility hanging over me.

To that end once the gates were closed there was zero access. I wasn't flexible on that no matter how much people begged because at the end of the day, it was all on my head. I turned back a couple who was visiting from China and on their last night arrived at the gates ten minutes after closing begging me to let them in. I said no. There were people coming in on transit whose buses were late and they missed the closing time. I said no. I felt like a complete asshole but last thing I needed was to have someone trip and fall and end up facedown in the memorial pool or down the ravine valley slope or any number of other hazards not visible in the dark. And I really didn't want to baby-sit them.

There was one exception.

Two teenaged girls came to the front gate about 20 minutes after closing one night. One girl was in tears because they knew the gates were already shut. They caught my attention as I sat in my car writing up my daily reports.

The girl that wasn't crying said, "You have to let us in. She needs to see her baby."

"Sorry, ladies. We have a strict rule for zero access after the gates have been closed. It's for safety and liability reasons."

"We know but it's the anniversary of her baby's death and she couldn't get off work in time to be here sooner. This will only take a minute."

The girl was sobbing. She was a mess. She looked up and brushed her hair away so she could see me and pushed a piece of paper through the bars of the gate. I grabbed it before she hit me in the chest with it. I turned so the entranceway overhead lights lit up the page. It was a newspaper clipping and I read it.

It was a story about a girl who'd been raped by her father and after the baby was delivered he strangled it before it could be put up for adoption. The girl and her mother testified against the father and sent him to jail.

I didn't know what to say. The other girl put her arm around the shoulders of the crying girl and looked at me. She was crying now as well. Fuck. These weren't girls at all but young women in pain. I unlocked the gate and let them in.

"Get in the car."

"You're a kind and wonderful man," the first one said.

They were both carrying flowers and I motioned for them to get in the back seat.

The woman who I assumed was the rape victim in the story began to compose herself. She reached over the back seat rest and handed me another piece of paper. It was the location of the plot for her baby. I studied it for a minute and checked it against my site map.

"This could be tough to find in the dark. Is there a marker or a headstone on the ground do you know?"

"It's a memorial wall plaque. I know exactly the place."

We drove off toward the area where her baby was interred. Fortunately it was in the section we were already in. Nobody spoke. It took about three minutes to get to the spot that was in a terraced area in the middle of the cemetery. I aimed the overhead spotlight at a wall full of memorial plaques.

"Look, I'll wait here for both of you and let you have some privacy. Please don't take too long. I could lose my job for letting you in here."

A million things immediately went through my mind. None of them pleasant. These are young women. One of them had already been raped. How much abuse preceded the death of this baby? Was she unhinged? Was I being punked? Was this a set up? Would this come back to bite me in the ass? I didn't know these women and this could be nothing more than an excuse to get me to let them into the cemetery. They might have just as easily run off to do some partying or whatever. I was getting uncomfortable with my own line of thinking and the thought of being responsible for their welfare.

I watched as they placed the flowers. The mother of the baby sat down and spoke out loud. It was out of earshot. I can't even imagine what she was saying. The other one stood and lit a cigarette and paced occasionally looking back toward me. She held up a finger after a while to indicate they'd be done in a minute. The mother stood up and the other girl hugged her. They turned and came back to the car.

The mother got in first and said, "Thank you, sir. You don't know how much this means to me. I don't know how I can ever repay you."

The other woman entered the car and I drove off toward the gates. I looked in the rear view mirror I could see the mother's eyes now, bloodshot, mascara everywhere.

All I could think of to say was, "I'm sorry about your baby."

"His name was Jacob." She leaned over the seat and kissed the side of my face. It was her thank you.

We got to the gate and I led them out of the car and into the night. They assured me they'd be safe getting home. I locked the gate and returned to the car where I sat and tried to finish writing my report. All I could do right then was wipe the side of my face. It was wet with tears.

LADIES OF THE NIGHT

With the exception of cyclists, hikers, joggers and a film crew that decided to became guerilla commandos and hide in one of the scattering forests while I was locking up one night (and caught them when I saw the battery indicator and LCD screen light up the side of a tree), I didn't get many oddball stragglers needing to be led out of the cemetery during closing time. There, of course, was always an exception.

People would often sneak up the ravine and into the tombstone valley before I locked up. They'd hide among the graves until I drove off and party as quietly as they could before subsequent patrols would uncover their shenanigans. I once encountered a street gang who'd taken up shop by some benches and to my utter surprise were quite courteous when I asked them to smoke their drugs elsewhere. They actually left in an orderly fashion and cleaned up their beer cans and food wrappers behind them. It could have turned out badly for me as I was outnumbered and trapped at the bottom of the valley with them.

Then there was the night I did a patrol along the top of the valley where the big captains of industry had their crypts and as the patrol car spotlight flitted across the top of the grass and among the monuments I caught a fleck of red sticking up from the valley's edge. I stopped the car and reversed so I could take another look.

I yelled out, "Security! The cemetery is closed."

Sure enough I saw a red head pop up from the edge of the hilltop. Then another head, this time blond, beside it.

"Great", I thought to myself. "Two people having sex on the side of the hill."

Now I'd have to get out of the car and confront them.

I repeated my lines, "Security! The cemetery is closed."

I could hear laughing and clearly see two people stumbling to try and get up the side of the valley incline.

"We need help here," one of them said.

As I got closer I could see it was a black woman with red hair about 6'5" tall in a striped red and black dress with her stiletto heels stuck in the grass being held up by a woman with a Billy Idol hairdo wearing a similar dress in white and black who was attempting to steady the two of them. She had one arm around the first woman and a full bottle of diet cola in the other. I suspected the cola was mixed with alcohol. I could smell it on both of them as I got near.

They laughed and jostled and stumbled their way toward me. "C'mon, ladies. Time to go."

"Ooo, look at this guy!"

"You ever fuck a security guard before, Linda?"

"He looks like a sailor. You can have him."

"Let's go, ladies. The gates are locked. I need to get you out of here."

"Can't we walk?"

"Clearly you can't," I retorted.

They both started to laugh.

"God, I'm so fucked up. Are you fucked up? Aren't you scared driving around in here?"

I stood by the car waiting for them to weave and dodge the imaginary obstacles they were facing and opened the back door of the patrol car.

"Hey, are we under arrest?"

"No, I'm just getting you back to the street. Which gate did you come through?"

"The one with the big ugly statue with the brass gargoyles. I think I fucked a few of those guys too."

They both laughed again and crumpled into the back of the car with the Amazon woman banging her head on the way in.

"Owwww!"

"Watch that," I said facetiously after she'd already done it.

I got in and we bolted. I drove very fast so I didn't have to listen to them talk…or throw up. We were at the gates in about 45 seconds flat.

"Holy shit, you're a fucking race car driver. Hey, Linda, have you ever fucked a race car driver?"

"Two. I think. In Montreal. That was a long time ago. They might have been cab drivers. They're sort of like race car drivers!"

The two laughed and laughed and rolled out of the car into the street.

"Safe trip home ladies."

As they stumbled away I heard one say to the other, "Hey, he didn't give you his tip. Hahaha!"

"Let's go get a drink."

And off they went.

CHAPTER ELEVEN

AND IN THE END

I handed in my resignation the week leading up to Labour Day weekend 2015. It was the culmination of a dozen different things. I had been mulling it over for a month really. Sitting in a patrol car for 15 hours a day making minimum wage was starting to wear me down – physically and mentally. It struck me hard that aside from the care of duty I prided myself in any monkey with a driver's license and a security license could do what I was doing. I came into the job with no discernible skills other than the ability to interact with the public. Something I actually loathed doing in reality. I'm not a people person but I managed to keep my interaction to a minimum working mostly alone and only dealing with people, for the most part one-on-one so there was never a complaint about my attitude - something that has plagued me my entire working life. The cemetery gig had actually taught me patience and tolerance for those whose life mission it was to exhibit copious amounts of disrespect, ignorance and a lack of common sense. I've never for a moment thought I was better than anyone else on the planet, I just couldn't stand being around people who, for whatever lame excuse, couldn't get their personal shit together. I don't suffer fools gladly.

Anyway, I knew my actual talents were being eroded and lost in this malaise of a daily grind. Watching others get on with their lives, having careers, being...happy. I was doing none of that. My family was suffering. They never saw me. I was coming home emotionally spent and fatigued every night. I would have divorced me had I been my wife.

Three events in quick succession tipped the scale in getting my ass out of a patrol car and back to working on things I was actually qualified to do.

One day out of the blue I got an email from someone asking if I'd been in the band Moving Targetz. I had. It was the group that gave birth to the record label I once owned but had to give up back when the recession destroyed the world economy. This gentleman ran a used record store where someone had attempted to pawn off what was effectively the master recordings of an album I'd done and several other tapes from artists I had on my label. I was both intrigued and panicked by this turn of events.

I knew who was trying to sell the tapes. My ex-landlord. When the axe came down on me and my family at the end of 2010 and our financial situation became unsalvageable we were evicted from the house we'd lived in for 11 years. We were grossly behind in the rent. We begged her for an extension so that we weren't out on the street at Christmas. She extended the execution date to January 31st, 2011. It bought us time to find a new home and get our stuff moved out. Fortunately, we found a place with a landlord who was very understanding to our plight. He was desperate to fill a vacancy in a single family house he owned that had been vacant since the summer. He was losing money every month the place stood empty.

Weather was bad through the early New Year and we had little money for movers. Friends helped us vacate. We ended up having to leave so much stuff behind as the landlord stood over us while we loaded out. She was there to change the locks. She also wanted her money or she was keeping what was still left in the house and that turned out to be the assets of my soon-to-be-closed record label.

I can discuss all day why I allowed this to happen but suffice it to say I was emotionally broken at that point. It had been a 4 year spiral into depression from the moment my father passed away in 2007 to that moment she asked me where the rest of her rent money was. I just wanted to get away from her, the building and the problem so I could look at it with fresh eyes down the road and come up with a solution.

None came. We continued to struggle financially and I never managed to get more than a handful of my belongings back from her over the next 4 years. In 2015 she decided she was going to sell her house and was liquidating my belongings to help raise funds to spruce it up and increase curb appeal.

As I found out from the used record guy, no one was buying the stuff from her. I thanked him and went to retrieve the master tapes a few weeks later. I feared, however, that she'd sell the house and toss everything she couldn't sell. I called her out of the blue.

At first she was defensive, lying to me about selling my stuff. I told her I wasn't mad. I wanted to work out how to get the record label archives back. She wanted the rent money that had been in arrears. No problem, I said. Give me 6 weeks. She agreed. At the beginning of August 2015 I launched a crowdfunding campaign to raise the money.

I decided then that I would also needed an exit strategy from my security job. I just wasn't sure when I should leave as I wanted to ensure I was still making an income through the planning stage of my next career decision. I also had to figure out if I would, in fact, re-launch the record label. The positive side was that vinyl records were having a resurgence and all my competitors had long since disappeared. I could just as easily make crap money from my home computer if I worked the same 15 hours a day I was wasting in a patrol car. The plan was set.

As the money started accumulating through the crowdfunding campaign from my amazing friends and supporters my daughter was going through some serious personal struggles. It was killing me that I couldn't be there for her. She was in crisis and internet emotional support was all I could offer. It was all being tossed at the feet of my ex-wife. There was an incident that got so bad I needed to leave and go get her. Except I would be fired if I left. She crashed and burned and I was trapped, stewing at the cemetery.

To my mother's credit she stepped in for me and went to my daughter's aid. I was angry at myself the rest of the day for being made helpless. It occurred to me that I should have left. I should never have had to make the choice because I would have been fired anyway I saw no reason to continue working for that company. I was damned if I did and damned if I didn't. Being damned on my own terms was something I was more than willing to take responsibility for.

I needed to discuss it with my wife. The night I went to have the conversation she injured herself doing a volunteer job that she loved. The injury put her in the hospital. She wasn't going to be able to work. With my son still in school there was no one to look after her until she recovered. I submitted my resignation the day after Labour Day weekend. I gave them two weeks notice. One year and one week after I'd been hired. They were not amused. I didn't care. I had family that needed me. I had a new career that I needed for my own mental health.

THE LAST DAY

My final day on the job was September 19, 2015. It was a Saturday.

Weekends were a little calmer, a little less officious because the office staff was reduced with only burials and viewings. The day wasn't particularly eventful. Or so I thought. Shortly before 6:30 PM when I'd already locked the maintenance yards and some of the vacated staff buildings I was about to settle in for my supper when a cyclist approached me saying there was a woman at the back of Section 1 in trouble. She'd locked her mother in the car. What?

I drove to where the woman was and sure enough, she'd gotten out of her van and accidentally left the keys to the van on the driver's seat – locking it absent mindedly behind her. In the passenger seat was her 92 year-old mother, strapped into a wheelchair and having zero independent mobility. Mom couldn't reach the keys or the door handle only inches away. And she was asleep.

This woman was pretty calm but certainly worried about getting back into the vehicle so they could leave. The sun was going down and the air was beginning to cool off. It was only a matter of time before the van itself became cold and Mom wasn't dressed for the occasion.

I had done my fair share of car break-ins at the rail yard the year before. Our drivers frequently dropped a door lock by mistake while jockeying vehicles. The problem with this woman's van though was that it was built like an armoured car. It was a rented disability vehicle that had most of the failsafe devices inside and outside removed – y'know, for the safety of the disabled person (what the hell?). I couldn't jimmy the windows to squeeze a coathanger in. The vehicle was vacuum-sealed. I couldn't go through the back hatch where the wheelchair ramp was as it had a roll bar that locked in place blocking door access while the vehicle was locked. It was a pickle.

I called the 1-800 number on the back of the van. As it

was a Saturday night, of course, they were closed. But their messaging system allowed me to leave a voicemail for the president of the company; the person that this lady had initially dealt with.

Time was ticking away. I was already going to miss my dinner and soon I would need to start locking down the cemetery to get it prepared for closing time.

She managed to get the attention of her mother who had been asleep until this point. She attempted to communicate through the double thick window but the old woman was both deaf and unable to respond back. They were both beginning to get anxious.

I called 911. I explained to them the situation and wondered if they could send a fire truck with equipment to pry open the vehicle or at least jimmy the window. Surely they had better equipment than I had. Dispatch promised a truck in two minutes. I was to meet them at the main gate and direct them in as the woman's vehicle was deep in the back of Section 1 and they'd need guidance. I told the woman I'd be back with help ASAP.

A police car arrived first and I gave the officers directions to the women and their van. The fire truck arrived less than a minute later except there was a problem. Remember when the cement truck ripped the front gate off? It still hadn't been fixed. The entire entrance was a concoction of temporary posts and snow fencing to give it a semblance of a secure entranceway. While it was being repaired they decided to just revamp the entire front gate system and put in some additional lighting. Half the driveway was missing and you could barely fit a car through what was left.

Just like the cement truck before it, the fire truck cut the corner too sharply coming in on Beacon Hill Road and snagged a piece of rebar – and the truck got stuck. Four studly He-Men firefighters jumped out and assessed the situation. The truck was now damaged and sitting on top of a mostly-bent piece of rebar. They tried backing up. The rebar punctured a back tire. The chief came over to me and just shook his head.

"Look, can my guys go in your car? I'll have to send for another vehicle to help us get the truck out of here." I waved at the other three firemen to come with me.

I opened the trunk of the patrol car and they dumped all their gear in. One of them got in the front with me, the other two in the back seat. Windows had to be rolled down so they had elbow room. Their overalls were bulky. One of the guys in the back still had an axe with him. They all had to squat in their seats because their helmets were rubbing the ceiling of the car. We now officially looked like the Keystone Kops.

We made the short journey to the back of Section 1 in about 40 seconds and rolled up behind the patrol car whose two police officers were also attempting to get into the van. They were having no luck either. The firemen rolled out and grabbed the gear from the trunk. They did an assessment of the van. They didn't have a window jimmy. Their tools were exclusively for aggressive entry – jaws of life, axes, utility belts.

Everyone's concern was focused on solving the issue as the 92 year-old occupant had now been locked in the van for an hour.

The fire truck finally pulled up behind us. One wheel flopping from the rupture. The chief jumped out and asked about the 1-800 number. I told him I'd called but they hadn't responded. He looked at the woman whose mother was locked inside.

"Ma'am, our only option here is to break through one of the windows in the van or pry a door open. Either way we'll damage the vehicle. We'd prefer not to especially knowing that your mother isn't in any real danger just inconvenienced and uncomfortable. Do you have a membership to the Automobile Association? They usually handle these kinds of calls. We'll step in if there's a medical issue, but this doesn't appear to be one."

"My purse is sitting on the front seat with my keys. The card is in there. I didn't think they'd come if I couldn't give them my membership number," she said in a defeated tone.

The police chief looked at me and asked if I could call CAA and get them to come out. I nodded and called my dispatcher to tell them the long tale and to get the number for CAA. I rang them on my cellphone and got an operator. I explained that it was a very unusual situation and that the woman could give them her name and address if they could match it to a registered membership. I handed the phone to the woman and she gave them details.

I stood and chatted with the emergency service guys. The police took a bow and headed off knowing they were no longer needed. She handed me back the phone. CAA confirmed a truck would be there to help out in less than 20 minutes. The firemen agreed to wait until the job was done.

I drove out to the front entrance again to meet the CAA driver and he was there in about 15 minutes. I escorted him to the back of Section 1. He got out, looked at the van, scrabbled around in a tool box in the back of the truck bed and had a large metal rod and a device that looked like a blood pressure cuff with a ball on it that you squeezed. It was the same gear we used at the rail yard. He had the firemen push on the driver side window to create a gap and proceeded to insert the flat cuff. Within seconds the cuff was inflated and he was able to insert the long metal rod in and popped the sliding door behind the driver's seat. He grabbed the handle and slid it back. We all cheered and applauded.

The woman opened the driver's door proper and pushed the locking mechanism to release all the locks in the vehicle. She then ran to the other side to check on her Mom. The old woman had fallen asleep again. It was a happy ending.

I was anxious to resume my rounds. I conferred with the firemen who were packed up and ready to leave and I said goodbye to the woman. She thanked me as well as all the responders that had helped. As I was getting back into my car my cellphone rang. It was the president of the company that owned the van.

"You were looking for me?"

I started to laugh and told him what had happened. He was embarrassed and told me to tell the woman to call him Monday where they would offer her a refund.

I said to him, "I will. And you might think about installing a failsafe on these vans. You got lucky this time that the 92 year-old lady wasn't in distress. We were minutes away from doing some serious damage to get her out of there."

He continued to apologize and said he would recommend a change.

The remainder of the shift was uneventful. I closed all the gates and said my farewells to the staff who were still cleaning up a memorial service at the Visitation Centre. I hadn't made a big deal about leaving. I know the staff liked me a lot there, but I didn't want them to make a hoopla about it. I had planned to visit one day again when I was no longer tied to a uniform.

I wrote up my lengthy report for the day's activity and dumped it in the mailbox beside head office along with my site cellphone. I did an inspection of the construction mess where the front gate used to be. It appeared that the rebar was now gone. The firemen had used a saw to cut off the top of it. The remaining stub – which was only a foot tall – had been bent sideways and out of the way of the driveway that was still accessible. Clearly these guys meant business.

I was left having to jerry-rig something to keep the front entrance closed. The rebar was now gone so I couldn't tie-off the snow fence that covered the hole where the gate used to be. I used a handful of Zip Ties to create a makeshift loop on the loose end of the snow fence. With considerable effort I managed to get the snow fence across the driveway securely by attaching it to a blinking construction light and blocked the driveway behind it with construction cones.

When I started the job at Beacon Hill I thought it odd that the dead were being jailed inside the cemetery with an 8-foot wrought-iron fence. Over the course of my time working there I learned that the fence was there to keep the living out. For a split second that night I had been tempted to just leave the gate open and let the Gods sort it out.

I didn't. The guard working the next day would have to deal with it and so I returned the site keys to the lock box. I turned the spotlight off on the patrol car and drove up Beacon Hill Road for the last time. I hung up my uniform that night and restarted my life running my own record label and spending time with my family again.

But the ghosts of Beacon Hill remain.

CHAPTER TWELVE

EPILOGUE

Since leaving my security guard job and the cemetery work that went with it I've been asked continuously to write the stories of my year there. I hope this book has satisfied those who have been curious about such things. It was tough to write and reliving what I consider to be some of the hardest days of my life. It has been therapeutic to an extent but opened a number of old wounds.

I left a lot of stuff out because it would have meant revealing the names of the actual cemeteries I worked at and the people that employed me. Those included a number of crimes that were reported in the news where employee names became public record.

Also, there were incidents involving specific deceased individuals whose anonymity was important to protect.

My apologies for not including those but I think it was more important to tell the human interest stories in a way that everyone can relate to without invading the privacy of the families. I do not want to encourage ghoulish cemetery scavenger hunting. Let the dead rest in peace.

Other reasons for omitting stories would have meant shaming or belittling individuals whose behaviour was truly inexcusable – much of it relating to race and religion. It was mind numbing to watch people carry hatred with them even after their loved ones had died.

I preferred not to give them a voice even in a fictionalized way.

PATROL CAR PLAYLIST

What I would like to share with you is a play list of the songs I was listening to in my patrol car. Talk radio was a good way to keep up on the daily news, but I'm a musician and preferred to fill my days with uplifting and reflective tunes while I wrestled with unleashed dogs and topless joggers. Here for your listening pleasure is my Top25 albums for long patrols.

1) Kris + Dee "A Great Long Game"
https://www.youtube.com/watch?v=Xg6Y7Z6PhG0

2) 54.40 "Casual Viewin'
https://www.youtube.com/watch?v=258Eutat9hM

3) Orson "Bright Idea"
https://www.youtube.com/watch?v=5i6Q-Ip4Uzk

4) Tears For Fears "Everybody Loves A Happy Ending"
https://www.youtube.com/watch?v=M2VLAa04pm0

5) Fastball "All the Pain That Money Can Buy"
https://www.youtube.com/watch?v=0jMyjjeSWak

6) Wings "Venus & Mars"
https://www.youtube.com/watch?v=OJnUIEvLYMc

7) Elton John "Captain Fantastic & The Brown Dirt Cowboy"
https://www.youtube.com/watch?v=gjEENn771G0

8) The Enemy "We Live and Die in These Towns"
https://www.youtube.com/watch?v=7miErQzz4Y8

9) Seal "Seal II"
https://www.youtube.com/watch?v=Mte99L-oOSY

10) Sugar Ray "Sugar Ray"
https://www.youtube.com/watch?v=xmLv8rfunPo

11) The Fixx "The Complete Fixx"
https://www.youtube.com/watch?v=ZCM4_5uB1ww

12) Rubber "Rubber"
https://www.youtube.com/watch?v=dPtw6NwKWlY

13) Paul Hyde "Big Book of Sad Songs, Volume 1"
https://www.youtube.com/watch?v=_f66R8NpIdM

14) The Alarm "Eye of the Hurricane"
https://www.youtube.com/watch?v=8D6pPgwafq0

15) Owsley "Owsley"
https://www.youtube.com/watch?v=dPjIJpsckng

16) Mike Previti "Extraordinary"
https://www.youtube.com/watch?v=cSr81ECuoKQ

17) Tom Hooper "Unexplored Cosmos"
https://www.youtube.com/watch?v=iekNFukU05k

18) Cheap Trick "Dream Police"
https://www.youtube.com/watch?v=Talf6QuVLLM

19) ELO "Out of the Blue"
https://www.youtube.com/watch?v=Y2h-2HQdTn8

20) Klaatu "Hope"
https://www.youtube.com/watch?v=elhTaC6jr88

21) Alan Parsons Project "I Robot"
https://www.youtube.com/watch?v=ONoi86Zyj3k

22) Supertramp "Breakfast In America"
https://www.youtube.com/watch?v=Yyqffz7K7aU

23) The Struts "Everybody Wants"
https://www.youtube.com/watch?v=ARhk9K_mviE&feature=youtu.be&t=62

24) Rational Youth "All Our Saturdays"
https://www.youtube.com/watch?v=LkKd_96Ovh0

25) Kongos "Lunatic"
https://www.youtube.com/watch?v=Gz2GVlQkn4Q

For more information about myself or the Cemetery Cop book, appearances, book signings, etc. check out these contact points:
http://www.cemeterycop.com
https://www.facebook.com/Cemetery-Cop-148271768946872/
https://www.facebook.com/jaimievernon
Baby raccoon video:
https://www.youtube.com/watch?v=DZQaanlzkso

Email: gwntertainment@gmail.com

Made in the USA
Columbia, SC
07 May 2017